GUILLAUME FAYE AND
THE BATTLE OF EUROPE

Published in the United Kingdom.

ISBN 978-1-907166-88-4

BIC classification:
Social & political philosophy (HPS)
Nationalism (JPFN)

Editor: Matthew Peters
Cover Design: Andreas Nilsson
Layout: Daniel Friberg

ARKTOS MEDIA LTD
www.arktos.com

MICHAEL O'MEARA

GUILLAUME FAYE
AND THE BATTLE OF EUROPE

ARKTOS
London
2013

To the Rising Generation,
Whose Great Deed will be the Soldier's Destiny

TABLE OF CONTENTS

War is the father of all things

— Heraclitus

INTRODUCTION:
WHY READ GUILLAUME FAYE

I did not come to bring peace but the sword.
— Matthew 10:34

In May 1945, Europeans lost the Battle of Europe. The Eastern half of the Continent fell to the Red Army, representing a Marxist rejection of European civilization — though one still adhering to certain of its traditions. The Western half fell under the suzerainty of the Americans — representing a *system* that had recently, and emphatically, thrown off the Christian civilizational forms that had burst forth a thousand years earlier under Charlemagne and then more enduringly under Otto I, but in both cases supported by the Catholic Church, the Continent's warrior nobility, and, until several generations ago, the vast majority of European peoples.

This American hegemon that came to dominate and Americanize postwar Europe first stepped onto the historical stage as a Janus figure — being both an extension of European civilization into the New World and an implicit Puritan rejection of the Old World (the *New* England). In the latter sense, Anglo-Europeans, 'traveling to the west for wealth or a new life', sought to escape their past (their family history) for a world without the burdens and corruptions imputed to their homeland.[1] To this end, the 'first new nation' cast off the hierarchy, community, and spirit of the Old World's Gothic Christianity, which contested its revolutionary New World Covenant with the god of Mammon.

From the marriage of Puritan radicalism and international capitalism, America's Reign of Quantity would issue forth and eventually assume world stature, once Roosevelt's War Deal bombed *Mitteleuropa* back to the Stone Age and incinerated a quarter million Japanese women and children with its newly concocted A-bomb — what the

---

1   Kathleen Burk, *Old World, New World: Great Britain and America from the Beginning* (New York: Atlantic Monthly Press, 2007), 2, 11, 44.

utterly mad Harry Truman called 'another weapon in the arsenal of righteousness'.[2]

Henceforth, America's 'global linear thinking', as Carl Schmitt was the first to observe, threw off its previous 'isolationist' contempt for the larger 'corrupt' world and gave itself over to the imperatives of its 'modern industrial-economic *Großraum*' (i.e., to its postwar development into an imperial market system based on the *nomos* it would soon impose on the 'free world').[3]

At the Nuremburg Trials (1945-46), this *nomos*, forged in the infernos of Dresden and Hiroshima, was formally enacted to replace the previous Westphalian system. The massacre of civilian masses — not entirely unknown in European history, but *never* condoned — was implicitly sanctioned. German 'war criminals' were tried on numerous *ex post facto* laws, but not for aerial bombardments in which hundreds of thousands of Europeans, mainly German women and children, perished under the most terrifying circumstances. Previous notions of *justus hostis* (a just enemy) and international law would eventually give way under the hegemon's dominion to a totalitarian unipolarity in which all challenges to American supremacy were to be treated as a threat to humanity itself. 'Human unity' would indeed replace the prerogatives of blood and spirit, for the *nomos* imbuing America with Providential powers posited 'the essential sameness of the human condition everywhere'.

The new forms — and hence rules — of this post-European, post-Christian counter-civilization, whose ideals stemmed from the marketplace, were 'structurally integrated' in subsequent decades on the basis of the premises worked out at Nuremburg — as other defining features of European civilization were replaced by forms and rules ultimately *legitimizing the mass murder of civilians* — as long as such mass murder served America's God-given mission in the world (most recently in Serbia, Iraq, and Afghanistan).[4] The country's inherent virtue, it is assumed, exempts it from all civilizing rule and principle. For it is always innocent. It is always right — as God's Chosen are meant to be.

---

2   Sacvan Bercovitch, *The American Jeremiad* (Madison: University of Wisconsin Press, 1978), 176-77.

3   Carl Schmitt, *The Nomos of the Earth in the International Law of the* Jus Publicum Europaeum, trans. G. L. Ulmen (New York: Telos Press, 2006 [1950]), 296.

4   Desmond Fennell, *Uncertain Dawn: Hiroshima and the Beginning of Post-Western Civilization* (Dublin: Sanas Press, 1996).

Following 1945, as the United States began organizing its world system in the name of free enterprise and democracy, *Europeans* were systematically deprived of their sovereignty, becoming, in effect, Washington's vassals. That U.S. hegemony coincided with an upturn of the economic cycle (what the French call 'the thirty glorious years') — stimulated by reconstruction, the Marshall Plan, and the 'transatlanticization' of Pentagon Keynesianism — meant that this vassalage came with certain material benefits, making it a condition of comfort, security, and even individual opportunity. Indeed, the materialism inherent in America's postwar system followed from its aspiration for a techno-scientific, distinctly this-worldly society devoted to entertainment, recreation, and sex. These 'cakes and ale' that came with postwar prosperity also made it difficult to complain about Europe's heteronomy within what Alexandre Zinoviev called the Cold War's *Global Suprasociety* — whose supranational amalgamation of European peoples into a single, American-dominated, military-economic bloc (as anticipated in the pre-war geopolitics of Nicholas Spykman and Isaiah Bowman, and planned early in the war as part of a larger imperial blueprint by the Rockefeller Foundation) was the crucial step in the development of its one-world market imperium.[5]

Not a colonial empire — though heir to Britain's strategy of dominating the sea lanes of global commerce, along with the world's money markets — the American system emerging from the war's holocaust was based on the financial and military supremacy that came with the postwar expansion of its permanent war economy.[6] The totally 'sensate' culture of this new imperial system, socially organized as a global, miscegenated consumer society, has dominated Western Europe and large parts of Europe's former overseas empires since 1945, and much of the rest of the globe since the Soviet collapse of 1991. Today, however, as the worm begins to turn, it is showing signs of breakdown — due, no doubt, to the contradictions and imbalances

---

5   Alexandre Zinoviev, *La grande rupture: Sociologie d'un monde bouleversé*, trans. Slobodan Despot (Lausanne: L'Âge d'Homme, 1999); F. William Engdahl, *Gods of Money: Wall Street and the Death of the American Century* (Wiesbaden: edition. engdahl, 2009), 136-65.

6   James Carroll, *House of War: The Pentagon and the Disastrous Rise of American Power* (Boston and New York: Houghton Mifflin, 2006); F. William Engdahl, *Full Spectrum Dominance: Totalitarian Democracy in the New World Order* (Wiesbaden: edition.engdahl, 2009).

inherent in its materialistic premises. The costs of these contradictions and imbalances have, in fact, already set off crises that will, should they converge, eventually threaten the system itself.[7] Since the financial meltdown of 2008, the 'cakes and ale' are gone. The system is now beset with economic decline, state indebtedness, massive disaffection (evident in the violent street clashes already disturbing Mediterranean Europe), and, most of all, the irresolvable problems created by the invasion of tens of millions of unassimilable, often hostile immigrants from the overpopulated South (encouraged in their colonization by the welfare apparatus of a Political Class, whose mediocrity and criminality are historically unprecedented). Such problems are at last starting to undermine the system's viability, as its dysfunctional tendencies become increasingly pronounced and its general course more and more like the proverbial runaway munitions train, speeding into the night.

Europe today seems headed toward another rupture in her history — one likely to involve institutional paralysis, general impoverishment, and possible ethno-racial upheaval. The leading academic authority on the breakdown of complex societies, Joseph Tainter, believes collapse is now foreseeable, and the former German Chancellor, Helmut Schmidt, fears that Europe has entered a pre-revolutionary period.[8] Worse, the prospect of such a collapse promises a situation potentially more cataclysmic than the last Battle of Europe, for it threatens not just another round of bloodshed and destruction, but ethno-civilizational clashes that will permanently compromise Europe's biocultural identity.[9]

This is the Battle of Europe for which Guillaume Faye is trying to prepare Europeans.

* * *

---

7 Philippe Grasset, 'Chaos pour chaos . . .' (October 1, 2012), http://www.dedefensa. org/article-chaos_pour_chaos_01_10_2012.html. The notion of 'sensate culture' (this-worldly and materialistic) comes from the work of Pitirim Sorokin; see his *Social and Cultural Dynamics*, 4 vols. (New York: American Book Company, 1937, 1941).

8 Joseph A. Tainter and Tadeusz W. Patzek, *Drilling Down: The Gulf Oil Debacle and Our Energy Dilemma* (New York: Springer, 2011); *Hamburger Abendblatt*, November 9, 2012.

9 Phil Williams, *From the New Middle Ages to a New Dark Age: The Decline of the State and U.S. Strategy* (2008), http://www.strategicstudiesinstitute.army.mil/pdffiles/pub867.pdf.

Faye is a French writer and social philosopher who has played a prominent role both in developing an anti-liberal critique of the prevailing system and in animating Europe's 'identitarian' resistance to it. He originally made a name for himself as a 'New Rightist' in Alain de Benoist's GRECE, France's leading anti-liberal 'think tank'. According to Robert Steuckers, the most erudite of the former New Rightists, Faye was the motor force of the New Right and its one original thinker.[10] Since leaving the GRECE in the late 1980s and then breaking with Benoist's increasingly system-friendly accommodations in the late 1990s, he has continued to speak and write, with the aim of averting another defeat in a war of which most Europeans were then largely unconscious.

In the various reviews, essays, and translations collected below, facets of Faye's project will be examined in greater detail.

Here, from a metapolitical angle, is why I think we should read Faye — if the above is not reason enough. I will start by mentioning that his last book, *Mon Programme* (2012), was a disappointment to his admirers — in no longer representing the cutting-edge of anti-system thought. But I believed the same of his *Nouvelle question juive* (2007), and then he wrote the remarkable *Sexe et dévoiement* (2011). He could conceivably still have other books in him that will need reading.

In any case, his present — let's say — less interesting turn, reflecting perhaps a certain intellectual stagnation, should not affect our appreciation of the visionary works he has already produced — which are just beginning, ten years later, to be translated into English — thanks to Arktos' campaign 'to make the world safe for Tradition'. Many of these works, remarkably, seem as pertinent to the situation today as when they were written — especially in the intellectual supports they lend to certain anti-system interventions.

In the first instance, Faye's 'literary' success as an anti-system critic owes much to what Patrick Pearse calls 'the vision and prophecy and the gift of fiery speech' that every great rebel has.[11] These qualities in Faye have enabled him to promote an understanding of the coming struggles that speaks to the anti-system tendencies now organizing the critical discourse on the reigning nihilism.

---

10 Robert Steuckers, 'L'apport de Guillaume Faye à la "Nouvelle Droite" et petite histoire de son éviction' (1995), http://robertsteuckers.blogspot.com.au/2012/01/lapport-de-guillaume-faye-la-nouvelle.html.

11 Patrick Pearse, 'The Rebel', http://www.youtube.com/watch?v=7wnqaSNygHs.

His rebel qualities may also have something to do with certain of his questionable allegiances, especially with Zionism — given that every rebel, especially in our degenerate age, tends to be his own law. One of Faye's friends describes him as an 'artist' with an illuminating imagination, like a sci-fi novelist, implying that (given his 'contradictions') he should be seen in artistic rather than political terms.[12] That may indeed be a useful precaution in approaching his ideas. But it should also be kept in mind that 'truth' assumes various forms and that great projects are often first announced as 'myth' or vision. In any case, Faye's visionary works are extremely political, even metapolitical, in summoning Europeans to the storms and struggles promising to sweep away the present spirit-killing system — and perhaps themselves.

* * *

Given the complexity of Europe's anti-liberal heritage — in its Traditionalism, anti-capitalism, anti-modernism, neo-paganism, traditional Catholicism, Heideggerianism, national-populism, identitarianism, regionalism, 'casapoundism', goldendawnism, neo-fascism, etc., as well as in its nationalist legacy and history of 'third way' tendencies — the New Right's two most important metapolitical contributions to the 'anti-system' forces challenging America's world order have been, in my view, (1) its alternative vision of the European project, and (2) its critique of the liberal dogmas governing the North Atlantic zone of the Americanosphere. Most else associated with the New Right is part of the anti-liberal heritage it has rescued from the soft totalitarianism programming Europe's obliteration.[13]

Both contributions have had a favorable impact on the European resistance, enhancing the effectiveness of its discourse and the appeal of its ideas. But neither the New Right 'pope', Alain de Benoist, nor its leading 'Protestant theologian', Guillaume Faye, has endeavored to systematize their anti-liberal critique into a specific political 'doctrine', as has the Russian New Rightist, Alexander Dugin, whose Fourth Political Theory is based on principles largely pioneered by

12 http://breizatao.com/?p=7010.

13 François-Bernard Huyghe and Pierre Barbès, *La Soft-idéologie* (Paris: Robert Laffont, 1987).

the French New Right, but unlike the French assumes the form of a single ideological worldview.[14]

There is nevertheless an *implicit* worldview in Faye's work. It comes from certain self-conscious metaphysical principles associated with his 'archeofuturism', along with his anthropological understanding of 'Man', his theory of the enemy, his strategy for negotiating the impending system collapse, and his tellurocratic conception of world order. But just as Faye's admired Nietzsche hated systems — the so-called bloodless artifices of dried-out minds — so too does he. For the sake of tracing the principal contours of Faye's thought, let me say something, next, about certain key ideas formative of his larger vision.

* * *

Perhaps the greatest challenge facing the anti-system movement is reconciling the legacy of the past, and all it implies about identity and destiny, with the imperatives of the future, which demand constant change and adaptation. Believing that notions of modernity and traditionalism need to be transcended, Faye proposes an *archeofuturist* 'philosophy' that approaches the future in the spirit of Europe's Faustian heritage.

At one level, this implies combining techno-scientific dynamism with the transmission of an archaic ethic uncorrupted by modernist belief in miracles and affirmative of the vital and originating in the European tradition. The archaic, in this sense, is not about conservatism, antiquarianism, or traditionalism, but about the transmission of foundational values that free the archeofuturist from the 'impasses of modernity'. (Remembrance of the year 732 A.D. thus prompts a daring assertion of Charles Martel's descendents in the year 2012.) The archaic, as such, imbues the European with an unsullied will and an originating instinct, which he applies to the challenges coming from the future.

At another, more existential level, Faye's archeofuturism implies Nietzsche's Eternal Return, in which European man throws off the follies of liberal modernity to resume his epic destiny in the spirit to which he was born. The archaic impetus for creation and

---

14 Alexander Dugin, *The Fourth Political Theory*, trans. Mark Sloboda and Michael Millerman (London: Arktos, 2012). The GRECE's *Manifeste pour une renaissance européenne* (Paris: GRECE, 2000) was an attempt, unsuccessful in my view, at a synthesis.

futurism's cutting-edge innovations connect in Faye somewhat in the way the Ancient Greek tragedians allied the Apollonian and the Dionysian — not for the sake of negating life's tragedies and trials, or forcing impossible synergies, but for a metamorphosis recapitulating the radical world-forming impetus of the European life force.

Who, though, is this European, who grows from the root of what has grown before? He is — in his authenticity — an offshoot of Europe's specific *bioculture*, a Fayian notion that conceives of man as a product of both his genetic and cultural heritage (like traditional Catholicism, which saw 'man as spirit and matter in one'): for though body and mind belong to different realms, they cannot exist without one another. Kill man's body and his spirit dies — and vice versa. Race and culture, blood and spirit, are inseparable. Europe's defense accordingly demands a self-assertion of her cultural tradition (the archeo) and a fanatical defense of her unique genetic heritage (the futurist). From this comes Faye's related notion of biopolitics, which aims at ensuring that Europe's biological/demographic imperatives are addressed, for a people's health and longevity depend, ultimately, on the vitality of its family forms and the reproduction of its population. A people's life is indeed primary, for everything else (culture, civilization, destiny) is premised on it.

Like any plant or animal, a bioculture (a people) needs its own habitat in which to thrive. Of necessity, it must exclude alien bloodlines and spiritual traditions that stunt, hamper, or threaten its own. One of the most menacing of these alien elements, according to Faye, is Islam's present colonization of Europe's historic biosphere.

For the reigning liberalism, peoples and nations are collections of individuals — all potential customers. Faye, by contrast, sees the intrusion of alien racial stocks and antagonistic civilizational forms not in terms of augmenting the population or developing the economy — but of destroying the nation, by replacing its original stock and undermining its native cultural forms. From this perspective, the system's anti-racism and Third World immigration are simply hastening the dissolution of Europe's historic identity. His prosecution by the French state for 'hateful incitement' in *La Colonisation de l'Europe* (2000), which warned of the Islamic invasion, made him for a time a symbol of the anti-system resistance. Unsurprisingly, he sees the main front in the impending Battle of Europe as forming before the invading Islamic hordes coming from the Global South.

However hideous the present anti-European system is becoming, there's still the possibility of redemption. Faye predicts it will come with system collapse (which, in Heideggerian terms, represents 'the midnight of the world's night', when danger reaches its peak and there 'grows that which saves'). For this sort of collapse — precipitated by the globalist destruction of Western economies, Third World colonization, and the irresolvable problems generated by the spreading chaos — will dispel illusion and bring about a state of emergency, automatically creating new possibilities to energize and concentrate the resistance. In positing an impending collapse that 'will consume the world in a great planetary chaos', his theory of the *convergence des catastrophes* offers not just an alternative to the existing system, it highlights the untenable premises upon which the present system rests: unlimited consumption, savage market practices, corruption and primitivization, the cannibalization of nature, family breakdown, the failure of cultural transmission and education, Third World overpopulation and First World senility, the privatization of the public and the socialization of private corporate incompetence, a foreign policy of violence and extortion, the dissolution of borders and historic identities, the mixing of incompatible peoples and religions, the ever deepening nihilism . . . The catastrophes created by these perverted practices, he predicts, will eventually converge in a civilization-wrecking collapse.

The good news is that only in such a truly catastrophic situation, with their backs against the wall, will Europeans think the 'unthinkable' and take those measures that in ordinary circumstance would be inconceivable. System collapse, ethnic civil war, and social breakdown — dire as these catastrophes will be — are the sole means by which Europeans will be forced to act. 'To construct a new home', Faye argues in *Why We Fight*, 'it's necessary that the old one collapses'.

To what end, then, will the coming Battle of Europe be fought? Foremost, of course, is the defense of Europe's genetic, cultural, and territorial legacies. Everything depends on that. But beyond that, the convergence promises the possibility of creating a new post-catastrophe order — a new civilization based on a different *nomos*. In Faye's Spenglerian-inspired vision, a post-nihilist Age of Faith and Authority could potentially emerge from the chaos of the now decaying civilization. Faye calls this new order *Euro-Siberia* — his mythic vision of an imperium of white 'European' nations and peoples, secure in their

native lands stretching from Galway to Vladivostok; politically federated according to the principle of subsidiarity, with an autarkic continental economy rejecting globalist free trade policies; and organized
not around the economy, like the EU and U.S., but as a civilizational
sphere linking the kindred peoples of Europe and Russia (the Boreans)
in an autonomous bloc decoupled from America's empire of consummate meaninglessness.[15] Following the coming era of world-changing
catastrophes, foreseen in his theory of convergence, such an envisaged 'empire of the sun', spanning 14 time zones, would, if realized,
constitute a Third Rome (which Russia alone never was) — becoming
thus a Great Fatherland 'in which the crystallization of the territorial
imperative' coincides with 'the ethnic imperative'.[16]

* * *

Graphic and compelling, his vision is not without problems, though it
has already armed Europeans with words and concepts that will help
them think through a possible recourse to their impending demise.

What are the problems in Faye's vision?

From my admittedly parochial perspective ('I should be dissatis-
fied in Heaven'), there are four major ones. The first has to do with
his understanding of archeofuturism, which tends to emphasize the
futuristic at the expense of the archaic. Dismissing (at time disdain-
ing) Traditionalist and Heideggerian reservations about technology,
Faye favors numerous techno-scientific tendencies he thinks necessary to European survival. Foremost of these are nuclear power,
genetic engineering, and a more general inclination to what is called
'transhumanism'. This 'ism' favors transforming the human condition by developing technologies that enhance human capacities and
overcome human limitations. I find this 'transhumanism' potentially
nihilistic, not only from the perspective of a 'Christian-European
rationality', which distrusts man's ability to improve on nature (for
'the sleep of reason brings forth monsters'), but also from a metahistorical perspective that sees the techno-scientific basis of our sensate
culture as having fixated on theories of truth that grasp only a narrow

15 Michael O'Meara, 'Liberalism as the Ideology of Consummate Meaninglessness'
    (2006), http://www.counter-currents.com/2010/09/liberalism-as-the-ideology-of-
    consummate-meaninglessness-part-1/.
16 Guillaume Faye, *Why We Fight: Manifesto of the European Resistance*, trans.
    Michael O'Meara (London: Arktos, 2011), 143.

aspect of human reality and consequently dismiss the most important things. The European tradition may be dynamically metamorphic, as Faye emphasizes, but without a sense of the 'sacred', the perennial source of all principle and value, life and society are unbalanced and ultimately untenable.

The second objection relates to Faye's notion of the 'enemy', integral to the Schmittian 'political'. For Faye, the greatest threat to European existence, Christian and secular, comes from Islam. If Europeans are to have a future (culturally, racially, or otherwise), he believes it will only come by excluding Muslims from their biosphere. In focusing, however, exclusively on the imminent (and undeniable) danger posed by Islamic civilization and its Muslim colonizers, Faye ignores or dismisses the globalist, Americanist, and liberal/financial forces responsible for infecting Europe with this alien pathogen. (Actually, to the degree that America has been one of Europe's many bad ideas — the fault originates in Europe.) American elites, it's well known, have long encouraged the Muslim colonization of Europe, for the sake of weakening her and have frequently used Islam as a proxy in their numerous world-engineering crusades, especially in its Wars of Ottoman Succession.[17] But most threatening, the system's totalitarian regime of political correctness straitjackets the European spirit and thus all possible resistance to its diabolical schemes for 'world betterment and brotherhood'. Faye's opposition to Islam's anti-European project fails, in a word, to address the system that makes possible the Islamic colonization.

Related to the primacy he attributes to Islam comes certain dubious foreign policy implications he draws from it. Seeing Israel as Islam's great enemy, Faye has come to embrace an essentially Zionist orientation that links Europe's fate to the 'Zionist entity' — which, of course, alienates him from those nationalists designating the Jews as the principal force of cosmopolitanism and race-mixing. Evident in the works he's produced since 2007, this Zionism also comes with an increasingly moderate stance toward the United States, the world's foremost anti-European power. His credibility in resistance ranks, not unrelatedly, has since plummeted.

---

17 Alexandre Del Valle, *Islamisme et États-Unis: Une alliance contre l'Europe* (Lausanne: L'Âge d'Homme, 1999); *Guerres contre l'Europe: Bosnie-Kosovo-Tchétchénie* (Paris: Éditions des Syrtes, 2000).

A fourth major criticism that can be made of Faye, this once brilliant student of the Jesuits, pertains to the anti-Christian paganism he inherited from Benoist's New Right. Its rejection of Christianity was actually one of the GRECE's most prominent and talked about features. Like *Grécistes*, Faye's critique, in stressing Christianity's moral egalitarianism, universalism, and individualism, is mainly a philosophical critique, indifferent to Christianity's role in having created and civilized Europe (as the *Respublica Christiana* grew into *Magna Europa*).[18] Implicitly, his rejection of Christianity (which conserved much of the Greco-Roman tradition) and, by implication, his rejection of its 'saintly, heroic, and ascetical ideals' follows the logic of modernity's naturalistic and capitalistic denial of transcendent truths — those 'truths' that make a people a people. Though Faye is wont to affirm his pagan beliefs, unlike a historic pagan (steeped in 'the idea of the Holy' and not merely its cognition), he pays little attention to what was or potentially remains hierophantic in Europe's tradition — in her sacred origin — but its recovery will alone save Europeans from modernity's enveloping nihilism.[19]

Since World War II, especially since the Vatican Council of 1962-65, when Marxists, Masons, and CIA fifth columnists like John Courtney Murray, S.J., captured the Church, *Novus Ordo* 'Catholicism' has been transformed into an objectively anti-European religion — whose ecumenical and ethnomasochistic evolution (toward the light of Liberation Theology, or, in its neocon variation, Milton Friedman) has created a new religion in radical rupture with all of Catholic tradition, as it converts to 'the false moral liberality of the Enlightenment' and its usurious system of capitalism.

From the perspective of the *longue durée* (for 1,500 years), Christianity has served as Europe's principal, most venerated spiritual form — and hence represents a complex, irreducible facet of the European heritage. Its history cannot be wished away or dismissed, for much of Europe's spiritual essence is intimately entwined in its Gothic Christian tradition, whose roots, not incidentally, lie deep in

---

18 Christopher Dawson, *The Making of Europe: An Introduction to the History of European Unity* (London: Sheed & Ward, 1946).

19 Rudolf Otto, *The Idea of the Holy*, trans. John W. Harvey (New York: Oxford University Press, 1958 [1923]); Michael O'Meara, 'Only a God Can Save Us' (2008), http://www.counter-currents.com/2010/07/only-a-god-can-save-us/; Martin Heidegger, *Contributions to Philosophy*, trans. Parvis Emad and Kenneth Maly (Bloomington: Indiana University Press, 1999 [1936-38]), §23.

the soil of Germanic, Celtic, and Greco-Roman paganism and whose Lord resembled not the Crucified, but the sword-wielding emperor, Charlemagne. It was the modern heresy of Protestantism, communicating vessel of capitalism and secularism, that Judaicized and de-Europeanized Christianity; Catholicism caught up with it in 1962. Both succumbed to the sensate, ultimately nihilistic precepts of liberal modernity, depriving Europeans of higher reference in an age of great spiritual confusion.

A categorical rejection of Christianity and its *complexio oppositorum* inevitably, then, rejects the larger heritage,[20] especially the communal, hierarchical, and sacramental spirit distinct to Catholicism's numinous imagination (Faustian in its High Culture and in the beauty of its rites).[21] And this, beware!, is no academic or religious matter, for Europeans will soon discover the Knight Templar in themselves, if they are to survive the coming Holy War. The secularization of certain Christian tenets — like universalism and equality — may have proven disastrous, but, *pace* the New Right, it is no fault of Christianity, but rather of a satanic system at war with Europe's sacred Tradition. I suspect the coming European Revolution will bear a cross of some sort on its banner: Celtic, hooked, or otherwise.

* * *

The essays, reviews, and translations collected below were produced over the last decade. I have arranged them chronologically for the sake of allowing the reader to follow Faye's evolution, as well as my own. Their different moods and interests inevitably reflect something of the period in which they were produced. And though I have re-edited these pieces for the sake of uniformity and made some stylistic changes, they appear largely as originally written.

San Francisco, November 2012

---

20 Carl Schmitt, *Roman Catholicism and Political Form*, trans. G. L. Ulmen (Westport: Greenwood Press, 1996 [1925]).

21 David Tracy, *The Analogical Imagination: Christian Theology and the Culture of Pluralism* (New York: Crossroad, 1987).

1

PREPARING FOR WORLD WAR III

Apropos of Guillaume Faye, *Avant-Guerre: Chronique
d'un cataclysme annoncé*. Paris: L'Æncre, 2002.

Readers of *The Occidental Quarterly* are probably unfamiliar with
the work of Guillaume Faye, but his ideas are increasingly those
of Europe's 'nationalist' vanguard.

An early associate of Alain de Benoist and one of the architects of
the European New Right, the young Faye left politics in the late 1980s
to pursue a career in media. Then, in 1998 he returned, immediately
re-establishing himself as *the* intellectual force on the anti-system
Right.

He has since published five books, each of which has had an impact
on the struggles against multiculturalism, Third World immigration,
and globalization.[1]

Unlike Benoist's wing of the New Right, which defends the European
ethnos solely on the cultural terrain, and unlike Le Pen's National Front,
which favors the assimilation rather then the forced repatriation of
non-Europeans, Faye claims race and culture are, at root, inseparable.
The struggle to preserve Europe's identity is thus for him a struggle to
defend not just the spiritual but the genetic integrity of its peoples.[2]

---

1   *L'Archéofuturisme* (1998); *Nouveau discours à la nation européenne*, 2nd ed.
(1999); *La Colonisation de l'Europe* (2000); *Pourquoi nous combattons* (2001). All
these works have been published by L'Æncre and can be purchased at the Librairie
Nationale, 12 rue de La Sourdière, 75001 Paris, or, on the internet, at www.
librairienationale.com [now defunct].

2   See my *New Culture, New Right: Anti-Liberalism in Postmodern Europe* (Bloomington:
1stBooks, In Press).

In this spirit, his latest work — *Avant-Guerre: Chronique d'un cata-clysme annoncé* (Pre-War: Report on an Impending Cataclysm) — bears a strong resemblance to Spengler's *Hour of Decision* (1934). For like Spengler, Faye scans the storms gathering on the horizon and foresees an era of world-altering tempests that will determine if Europeans are to have a future or not.

These storms, he claims, will be neither ideological nor economic in character, but racial and civilizational (*à la* Huntington), involving clashing continental blocs and warring ethno-racial groups. Though totally unprepared for the violence and destruction they will unleash, he believes these conflicts will nevertheless give Europeans on both sides of the Atlantic a final chance of throwing off the stupefying forces that have denatured them for the last half century.

Europe and America

Like most 'new nationalists' opposing the U.S./EU's one-worldism, Faye is extremely critical of the U.S. government and its unrelenting assault on the cultural and biological foundations of white European life. But he parts company from many anti-Americans in believing that the U.S. is not Europe's principal enemy (even if he acknowledges that its New Class has contributed much to Europe's present debilitation). An enemy, he contends, does more than corrupt, exploit, and reduce one's heritage to the cartoon images of America's Culture Industry: above all, it threatens one's life. Taking his cue from Carl Schmitt, Faye thinks it is more accurate to characterize the U.S. as Europe's 'adversary' — i.e., as a force that needs to be resisted if Europeans are to reassert the destinying project distinct to their *ethnos* — but nevertheless one with whom a life-and-death struggle is not at all inevitable.

Europe's real enemy, he argues, is Islam and its metastasizing European presence. *Avant-Guerre* is accordingly something of a jeremiad against the anti-European implications of the Prophet's faith.

Yet if the billion Muslims seething on the Continent's southern and southeastern borders and the millions already settled within its borders menace Europe's existence, they are, paradoxically, not America's enemy. Based on the work of General Pierre-Marie Gallois, Alexandre Del Valle, and a new generation of European geostrategists, Faye argues that until quite recently Islam has played a leading role in furthering the hegemonic ambitions of America's global village. That its recruitment of jihadists to fight in Afghanistan and Chechnya, Bosnia and Kosovo, at last boomeranged ought not to detract from the fact that since 1979, U.S.-incited insurgencies in the Muslim world have strategically served the geopolitical imperatives of its Cold War, petroleum, and, pre-eminently, Zionist interests. The Bush Administration's present Likudization and the Second American War on Iraq (both of which occurred after *Avant-Guerre*'s publication) will certainly affect Faye's view and compel him, perhaps, to modify his argument. But however revised, the work of this European patriot demands our utmost attention.

Looking in our direction, he warns that America's principal enemy, and the threat it will face in the next war, comes not from the Middle East (even if its fundamentalists continue to target the United States), but from a rapidly developing and technologically sophisticated China bent on contesting U.S. hegemony over those Pacific regions historically linked to the Chinese mainland and its civilizational sphere. In this potential Sino-American conflict, he believes the future lies entirely on the Chinese side. For unlike the Middle Kingdom, an ethnic empire of ancient lineage, the U.S. is a *symbiose étatico-entrepreneuriale*, with a colorless population loyal only to a paycheck, an economic opportunity, or a particular life-style, but not to a destinying project rooted in blood and history. This bureaucratic/capitalist enterprise inspired by the Jacobin ideology of global markets and global integration, he predicts, is likely to fracture into rival segments, if challenged by a determined enemy. In the great struggles ahead, it will fall, as a consequence, to Europe — a Europe ideally allied or federated with Russia — to defend the white homelands from the ever-encroaching Third World.

Islam

If America faces the prospect of an interstate war with China, Faye predicts that Europe faces an intrastate conflict (a 'Fourth Generation War') with an insurgent Islam — a conflict similar to what the Israelis encountered in South Lebanon a decade ago.

Since 1962, when Africa broached Europe's southern frontier, the Continent, especially France and Belgium, has been inundated by successive waves of Third World immigrants. Involving masses and not individuals, the amplitude of this immigration is such that not a few demographers describe it as a 'colonization'. The non-white, largely Muslim, and unassimilable invaders are, in fact, already beginning to 'de-Europeanize' Europe. Virtually everywhere they have settled they have 'ethnically cleansed' local populations, establishing not ghettos, but conquered territories, from which future conquests are presently being prepared.

This is creating an extremely volatile situation, for Europe lacks the massive police apparatus and the geographical expanses that keep ethno-racial tensions 'manageable' in the U.S. Typically, in French urban areas, where neighborhoods have been lost to Islamic civilization, Europeans experience not just escalating levels of violence and insecurity, but the loss of their laws and institutions. There are now 1,400 *zones de non-droit* in France (including 11 towns) and in nearly a hundred of these, republican jurisdiction has given way to *shari'a* (Islamic law).[3] Conditions in these *zones*, which politically correct officials persist in describing in socioeconomic rather than biocultural terms, are such that it's become impossible for a Frenchman to reside in the public housing estates (HLM) built for the French working class, find a café serving wine or ham, or have his wife dress or behave as a European women. More seriously, these non-European enclaves have not the slightest intention of assimilating into the *Dar-al-Harb* (the 'impious' non-Islamic world, which Muslims view as a 'world of war') and have begun, in small and increasingly not so small ways, to assert their autonomy from it. Hardly a week passes now without a news report of a riot or bloody clash between police and Muslim gangs.

In face of this de-Europeanizing immigration, the media, the academy, and the established 'anti-racist' organizations (most controlled by Zionists) glamorize the term 'multiculturalism', associating it with the mobile postmodern society of optional values and fashionable identities that comes with globalization. But more than

---

3   Jeremy Rennher, 'L'Occident ligoté par l'imposture antiraciste', *Écrits de Paris*, no. 640 (February 2002). Even the politically correct editor of *Violence en France* (Paris: Seuil, 1999), Michel Wieviorka, acknowledges that the explosion of violence and criminality since 1990 is an outgrowth of Islamic power. Because the French government keeps most data on immigrant crime and racial terror securely under wraps, the little that is known has been surreptitiously leaked by frustrated officials. The publication with the best access to these leaks is the monthly *J'ai tout compris! Lettre de désintoxication*, edited, not coincidentally, by Guillaume Faye.

undermining the legitimacy of European culture, they ruthlessly seek to criminalize whoever criticizes their ethnocidal policies. Instead, then, of mobilizing the Christian West against the dangers threatening it, these New Class forces preach cowardice, resignation, escapism, and a suicidal humanitarianism.

At the same time, the regnant elites persist in distinguishing between violent fundamentalists (who number perhaps 40,000 in France) and the 'peace-loving' Muslim community, stupidly ignoring Islam's inherent hostility to the racial-cultural character of European peoples. Between orthodox and fundamentalist Islam, Faye insists, there is only a difference in temperament, for both are inherently anti-European. Years before the 9/11 attack on the symbols of U.S. hegemony, this 'monstrous offshoot of Judaism' began a third great offensive against the *Dar-al-Harb*, targeting Europe as a future Muslim homeland.[4] Buoyed up by U.S.-protected strongholds in Southeast Europe (Albania, Bosnia, Kosovo), aggressive U.S. lobbying to admit Muslim Turkey to the EU, and sophisticated arms stockpiled in thousands of Saudi-financed mosques, Islamicists are visibly preparing the way for a new conquest.

It is not surprisingly, then, that Faye interprets the growth of European Islam as a dire threat to European existence.[5] His hostility to Islam ought not, however, to be confused with that of President Bush's handlers. The struggle against Islam, he insists, is a struggle for Europe's survival — not justification for further U.S./Zionist aggressions.

What War Will Bring

In the coming cataclysms — likely to involve street battles between racial communities, guerilla skirmishes, mega-terrorism, perhaps even small-scale nuclear exchanges with 'dirty bombs', along with the possibility of conventional-style invasions from neighboring Islamic

---

4   The first Arab wave of the Eighth century brought the Muslims to Poitiers and the second Turkish wave of the Twelfth-Seventeenth centuries led to the destruction of Christian Byzantium, the occupation of Southeast Europe, and the storming of Vienna. The third wave, in the form of the present colonization, is more stealthy in character, but potentially more catastrophic.

5   Not a few nationalists now invoke the need for a new *Reconquista*, evident in Philippe Randa's novel *Poitiers demain* (Paris: Denoël, 2000) and the album *Reconquista* by the group Fraction on Heretik Records.

states (Turkey, for instance, has the largest, most powerful army in NATO, after the U.S.) — Faye believes Europe will either perish, passively resigning herself to the present de-Europeanization, or else experience a rebirth in which she will reclaim the grandeur of her ancestral heritage. In either case, the present politically correct illusions will eventually be forced to give way to more primordial truths.

Like every struggle affecting a people's natural selection, war privileges the elemental and the vital. With it, the subtle distractions that sophists and simulators use to mislead Europeans, as well as those minor narcissistic differences that continue to divide them, are likely to cede to the higher imperatives of survival. For in such a situation, the present cosmopolitan elites, like their former Soviet counterparts, are likely to be swept aside by a new leadership dedicated to Europe's destiny.

The situation Europeans find themselves in today may therefore be unconditionally bleak, but in that hour when everything risks being lost, Faye believes a final opportunity for renaissance will arise.

In this spirit, he claims the dominant musical theme of the Twenty-first century will be neither an orchestral ode to joy nor the doggerel of an urban savage, but rather a solemn military march based on ancient airs. Europeans on both sides of the Atlantic, he leaves unsaid, would do well to keep step with its strong, marked rhythms.

The Occidental Quarterly 3, no. 2 (Summer 2003)

2

ETHNONATIONALISM VERSUS COMMUNITARIANISM: THE FAYE-BENOIST DEBATE

TRANSLATOR'S INTRODUCTION: *As part of the controversy over Jacques Chirac's decision to ban the Muslim headscarf in French public schools, the following pieces by Alain de Benoist and Guillaume Faye appeared in the review* Terre et Peuple, *one of the many split-offs from the Groupement de Recherche et d'Études pour la Civilisation Européenne (GRECE). Founded in 1968, the anti-liberals identifying themselves as* Grécistes *believed the American-centric order imposed on Europe in 1945 — with its miscegenational social practices and the capitalist 'totalitarianism of its* Homo dollaris uniformis' *— would never be overturned as long as its opponents appealed to the discredited political legacies of Vichy, colonialism, Catholicism, monarchism, or neo-fascism, all of which had failed to make the slightest impact on the postwar era. Taking a page from the Left's playbook, the GRECE's young founders abandoned these earlier forms of anti-liberalism for a 'Gramscianism of the Right', which aimed at metapolitically subverting the liberal order at the level of culture and belief.*

Given the egalitarian principles undergirding liberalism's anti-nationalist worldview, the 'biological realists' of the early GRECE sought to popularize what contemporary science had to say about 'human equality'. Their anti-egalitarian metapolitics failed, however, to influence the dominant discourse, which brooked not the slightest abridgement of this cardinal principle. Once this was evident, Grécistes began rethinking their cultural strategy and the need to pursue a less

26

confrontational approach. In doing so, they gradually downplayed, then discarded, their biological realism for the sake of an 'ethnoplural- ism', which endeavors to legitimate white racial identity in the name of cultural heterogeneity (another term for 'diversity'). This new strategy was premised on the belief that ethnopluralism, whose principle of self- determination had gained prominence in the decolonization and anti- imperialist movements of the previous decades, could be used to defend the racial/cultural integrity of European peoples, for if Third World peoples had the right to self-determination, then, it was reasoned, so too did Europeans.

The GRECE's ethnopluralist turn took the form of two slogans: la droite à la différence *and* la cause des peuples, *both of which trans- late awkwardly into English, but which imply that humanity 'can only remain healthy as long as cultural diversity is safeguarded' from the homogenizing forces of the global market (the right to difference) — and as long as every people retains the right to assert its distinct cultural identity (the cause of the peoples). Then, as these slogans penetrated the larger nationalist movement, Le Pen, Haider, Fini, and numer- ous nationalist parties and groupuscules across the Continent soon employed some variant of these slogans to justify their defense of Europe's unique bioculture. The success of such efforts also seemed to suggest that it was wiser to promote European survival on the basis of agreement than on conflict, for in using slogans congruent with liberal beliefs, even if they broke with liberal goals, anti-liberals would be able to exploit the dominant discourse for their own cause. Or so the theory went.*

*This brings us to Guillaume Faye. With a pen as mighty as his former comrade, he now challenges Benoist's claim that Third World immigration has become an undeniable, and hence uncontestable, facet of European existence and that it must be dealt with in ways recognizing it as such, and not terms of a self-defeating ethnoplural- ism. Like a number of prominent early ex-*Grécistes *(such as Robert Steuckers, Pierre Vial, Pierre Krebs, etc.), Faye continues to write, speak, and agitate in defense not simply of Europe's cultural and communal heritage, but of the ethno-racial homogeneity of its lands. He thus rejects all compromise with liberal egalitarianism, aligning himself against the GRECE's 'differentialist' discourse. For in assum- ing the liberal postulates underpinning the politics of ethnopluralism, Faye claims the GRECE has become increasingly complicit with the* *governing elites, whose own variant of ethnopluralism justifies the ongoing de-Europeanization that comes with open borders and free trade. — M.O.*

Interview of Alain de Benoist
From *Terre et Peuple*, no. 18 (Winter Solstice 2003)

Terre et Peuple: The present dispute [over whether Muslim females will be allowed to wear the veil in the classroom] has revived the question of communitarianism. In numerous books and articles published over the years, particularly in the columns of *Éléments* [the GRECE's popular trimestrial review], you have frequently taken positions at odds with your readership. I would like to begin this interview by asking if there has been any fundamental changes in our society in the years [since the Cold War's end, when last you took a public stand on this issue], and, by contrast, if the identitarian movement is not better situated today to address this disturbing but crucial dispute.

Alain de Benoist: I've always taken positions contrary to those who don't know or understand my own. But I'll admit I have displeased some in saying that immigration is a fact, no longer an option, and that in engaging a battle, one has to fight on its specific terrain, not on the one which we might prefer to fight . . .

What's happened in the last fourteen years? The social pathologies engendered by a massive, uncontrolled immigration have gotten incontestably worse. These pathologies have made life more difficult for millions of people, who see no likely end to their difficulties. One consequence of this has been a certain shift in perspective. The comforting idea of a future *Reconquista* [in which Europeans will militarily recapture the lands now lost to Third World immigrants] is no longer entertained, except by a handful of spirits who haven't a clue as to what world they're living in. At the same time, no one (with perhaps the exception of the business class) proposes a further opening of our border — which, in any case, no longer stops or guarantees anything. If the question of the veil has aroused such heated discussion, it's only because it provides the political class a convenient way of dealing with a problem that it has refused to address. But however it is posed, there's likely to be no end to this dispute. For my part, the position I took on the subject in *Le Monde* in 1989, when it was still possible to write [for France's 'paper of record'], has not changed.

Terre et Peuple: The communitarian phenomenon encompasses many diverse realities (or at least the appearance of them): communities formed by non-European immigrants, communities based on religious affiliation, sexual preference, or regional identities, all of which are now experiencing a revival . . . But are these communities of comparable worth? For a communitarian, is it necessary to legitimate every community in the name of the *droit à la différence*?

Alain de Benoist: Let's begin by clarifying our terms. First, there is the notion of community, which Ferdinand Tönnies developed in opposition to the concept of society. Unlike society's mechanical [or functional] relations, in which social organization is based on individuality and individual interests, community defines a mode of organic sociality. In Max Weber's term, this notion is an ideal type, for every collectivity, in different proportions of course, possesses traits that are distinct to both community and society. Based on Tönnies' work, but with reference to Aristotle, there has arisen a communitarian school of thought, whose principal representatives are Alasdair MacIntyre, Charles Taylor, and Michael Sandel. This school highlights the fictitious character of liberal anthropology, insofar as liberalism posits an atomized individual who exists anterior to his ends, that is, an individual whose rational choices and behavior are made and motivated outside a specific sociohistorical context. For the communitarian, [by contrast, the extra-individual forces of larger social or communal ties] are what constitute and motivate the individual. Identity, thus, is that which we choose to be before we even recognize who we are, being the inherited framework which defines the horizon of our shared values and lends meaning to the things of our world. As a specific moral value, then, identity is anterior to any universal conception of justice — although the liberal believes such a conception ought to trump every particularistic sense of the good.

Terre et Peuple: Doesn't the communitarian's systematic legitimation of difference lead to an impasse? Indeed, don't certain communities refuse difference or seek to impose their will on others once they become dominant? In the name of difference, doesn't one ultimately risk denying one's own difference?

Alain de Benoist: The recognition of difference is not necessarily angelic in its effects. It also doesn't eliminate conflict. The right to difference or to an identity is much like the right to freedom: its abuse simply discredits its usage, not its principle. In this I oppose [the feminist philosopher] Elisabeth Badinter, who, in justifying 'the right to indifference', assumes that every time we emphasize 'our differences at the expense of our common ties, we create conflict'. Common identities can, in fact, be just as conflictual as differences: think of the 'mimetic rivalry' that [the literary scholar and anthropologist] René Girard has analyzed. A recognition of differences doesn't do away with the need for a common body of laws (which, indeed, is prerequisite to it) nor is it necessarily incompatible with notions of citizenship or the common good. The state's duty is to ensure public order, not to incite hatred. Similarly, a policy recognizing difference demands reciprocity. He who designates me as his enemy becomes my enemy. For whoever promotes his difference in denying mine, abrogates the principle's generality. It is thus necessary to create a condition in which our reciprocal differences are recognized, which isn't possible once immigration, Islam, fundamentalism, and terrorism are lumped together.

In respect to 'the right to difference' [*la droit à différence*], it is necessary to dispense with certain equivocations. First, it is a question of right, not an obligation. In recognizing difference, we create the possibility of living according to those attachments we consider essential, not for the sake of enclosing ourselves in them or keeping them at a distance. Difference, moreover, is not an absolute. By definition, it exists only in relation to other differences, for we distinguish ourselves only *vis-à-vis* those who are different. The same goes for identity: even more than an individual, a group does not have a single identity. Every identity is constituted in relationship to another. This also holds for culture: for in creating its own world of meaning, a culture nevertheless does so in relationship to other cultures. Different cultures are not incomparable species, only different modalities of human nature. Let's not confuse the universal with universalism.

Terre et Peuple: In your opinion, is communitarianism an effective response to the problems created by the introduction of millions of non-Europeans into Europe? Indeed, isn't community important because it is a function of its specific place and time? For instance, there exist communities that are more rather than less dynamic, especially in terms of natality. Given the failure to integrate non-Europeans, the utopia of a *Reconquista*, and a communitarianism cloaking a demographic time bomb, isn't this enough to make one pessimistic?

Alain de Benoist: First, let me say that whenever men fail to find a solution to their problems, history finds one for them. Second, history is always open (which doesn't mean that everything is possible). Finally, in posing a problem in a way that has no solution, it shouldn't be surprising that one is condemned to pessimism. Today, in Europe there are 52.2 million Muslims (25 million in Russia and 13.5 in Western Europe), a majority of whom are of European stock [*sic*]. The rest, as far as I know, are neither black nor Asian. If Europeans are less demographically dynamic, it is not the fault of those who are. If they no longer know what their identity is, again this is not the fault of those who do. In face of peoples with strong identities, those lacking such an identity might reflect on why they have lost their own. To this end, they might look to the planetary spread of market values or the nature of Western nihilism. In an era of general deterritorialization, it might also be useful to think of identity in ways that no longer depend on locale. For my part, I attach more importance to what men do, than to what they presume themselves to be . . .

Guillaume Faye: 'The Cause of the Peoples?'
From *Terre et Peuple*, no. 18 (Winter Solstice 2003)

The [GRECE's] *cause des peuples* is an ambiguous slogan. It was initially conceived in a polytheistic spirit to defend ethno-cultural heterogeneity. But it has since been recuperated by egalitarian and human rights ideologies, which, while extolling a utopian, rainbow-colored world order, seek to inculpate Europeans for having 'victimized' the Third World.

Failure of a Strategy

When [GRECE-style] identitarians took up the *cause des peuples* in the early 1980s, it was in the name of ethnopluralism. This 'cause', however, was little more than a rhetorical ruse to justify the right of European peoples to retain their identity in face of a world system that seeks to make everyone American. For in resisting the forces of deculturation, it was hoped that Europeans, like Third World peoples, would retain the right to their differences [*la droit à la différence*] — and do so without having to suffer the accusation of racism. As such, the slogan assumed that every people, even white people, possessed such a right. But no sooner was this argument made than the cosmopolitan P.-A. Taguieff [a leading academic commentator on the far Right] began referring to it as a 'differentialist racism' [in which cultural difference, rather than skin color, became the criterion for exclusion].

In retrospect, the New Right's strategy seems completely contrived, for *la cause des peuples, la droit à la différence*, and 'ethnopluralism' have all since been turned against identitarians. It is, moreover, irrelevant to Europe's present situation, threatened, as it is, by a massive non-European invasion and by a conquering Islam, abetted by our ethnomasochistic elites.

Recuperated by the dominant ideology, turned against identitarians, and rendered tangential to current concerns, the GRECE's ethnopluralist strategy has been a metapolitical disaster. It also retains something of the old Marxist and Christian-Left prejudice about Europe's 'exploitation' of the Third World. As [the French Africanist] Bernard Lugan shows in respects to black Africa, this prejudice is based on little more than economic ignorance. The *cause des peuples* is nevertheless associated with a Christian-like altruism that demonizes our civilization, which is accused of having destroyed all the others, and does so at the very moment when these others are busily preparing the destruction of our own civilization.

The 'right to difference' . . . What right? Haven't we had enough Kantian sniveling [about abstract rights]? There exists only a *capacity* to be different. In the selective process of History and Life, everyone has to make it on his own. There are no benevolent protectors. This right, moreover, is applied to everyone but Europeans, who, [in the name of multiculturalism or some other cosmopolitan fiction], are summoned to discard their own racial/cultural identity.

This slogan poses another danger: it threatens to degenerate into a doctrine — an ethnic communitarianism — sanctioning the existence of non-European enclaves in our lands. For in the Europe this communitarianism envisages, communities of foreigners, particularly Muslim ones, will, for obvious demographic reasons, play an ever-greater role in our lives. This affront to our identity is accompanied by sophistic arguments ridiculing the 'fantasy' of a [possible white] *Reconquista*. In this spirit, we are told that we will have to make do [with a multiracial Europe]. But I, for one, refuse to make do. Nor am I prepared to retreat before an alleged historical determinism [which aims at turning Europe into a Third World colony].

The *cause des peuples* is now part of the human rights vulgate. By contrast, the neo-Darwinian thesis of conflict and competition, which assumes that only the fittest survive, seems to our bleeding-heart communitarians a vestige of barbarism — even if this vestige accords with life's organic laws. Given its recognition of selection and competition, this thesis alone is able to guarantee the diversity of life's varied forms.

The *cause des peuples* is also collectivist, homogenizing, and egalitarian, while the 'combat of peoples' is *subjectivist* and heterogeneous, conforming to life's entropic properties. In this sense, only nationalism and clashing wills-to-power are capable of sustaining the life-affirming *principle of subjectivity*. The egalitarian supposition that every people has a 'right to live', the *cause des peuples* prefers to ignore obvious historical realities for an *objectivism* that endeavors to transform the world's peoples into objects suitable for a museum display. It implies, as such, the *equivalence* of all peoples and civilizations.

This sort of egalitarianism assumes two basic forms: one offers a homogenizing but *metissé* concept of what it means to be human (the 'human race'), the other seeks to preserve peoples and cultures in a way a museum curator might. Both forms refuse to accept that peoples and civilizations are *qualitatively* different. Hence, the absurd idea that one has to save endangered peoples and civilizations (at least if they are Third World) in the same way one might save an endangered seal. History's turbulent selection process, though, has no room for *preservation* — only competing subjectivities. In its tribunal, Salvationist doctrines are simply inadmissible.

The *cause des peuples* also assumes an underlying solidarity between European and Third World peoples. Again, this is nothing but a dubious ideological construct, which *Grécistes* invented in the early Eighties to avoid the accusation of racism. I don't have the space here to expose the myth of Third World 'exploitation'. However, to explain its misfortunes in crude neo-Marxist terms, as if it were due to the machinations of the IMF, the Trilaterals, the Bilderberg Group, or some other Beelzebub is hardly worthy of a response.

Europe First!

If our communitarians really want to defend the *cause des peuples,* they might start with Europeans, who are now under assault by the demographic, migratory, and cultural forces of an overpopulated Third World. In face of such threats, you won't find me sniveling like a priest or fleeing like an intellectual to the 'Other's' cause: 'Ourselves alone' will suffice.

National Vanguard, May 11, 2004

3

THE WIDENING GYRE

Apropos of Guillaume Corvus, *La Convergence des catastrophes*. Paris: Diffusion International, 2004.

Nearly three hundred years ago, the early scientistic stirrings of liberal modernity introduced the notion that life is like a clock: measurable, mechanical, and amenable to rationalist manipulation. This modernist notion sought to supplant the traditional one, which for millennia held that life is organic, cyclical, and subject to forces eluding mathematical or quantifiable expression. In this earlier view, human life was understood in terms of other life forms, being thus an endless succession of seasons, as birth, growth, decay, and death followed one another in an order conditioned by nature. That history is cyclical, that civilizations rise and fall, that the present system will be no exception to this rule — these notions too are of ancient lineage and, though recognized by none in power, their pertinence seems to grow with each new regression of the European biosphere. With Corvus' *Convergence des catastrophes*, they assume again something of their former authority.

'For the first time in its history', Corvus writes, 'humanity is threatened by a convergence of catastrophes'. This is his way of saying that the Eighteenth-century myth of progress — in dismissing every tradition and value distinct to Europe — is about to be overtaken by more primordial truths, as it becomes irrefutably evident that continued economic development creates ecological havoc; that a world system premised on short-term speculation and financial manipulation

35

is a recipe for disaster; that beliefs in equality, individualism, and universalism are fit only for a social jungle; that multiculturalism and Third World immigration vitiate rather than revitalize the European homelands; that the extension of the system's so-called republican and democratic principles suppress rather than supplant the popular will, etc. In a word, Corvus argues that the West, led by the United States, is preparing its own irreversible demise.

Though *Convergence des catastrophes* takes its inspiration from the distant reaches of the European heritage, its actual theoretical formulation is of recent origin. With reference to the work of French mathematician René Thom, it first appeared in Guillaume Faye's *L'Archéofuturisme* (Paris: L'Æncre, 1998), arguably the key work of the 'new European nationalism'. Indeed, those familiar with his style and sentiments are likely to suspect that 'Corvus' is Faye himself.

Anticipating today's 'chaos theory', Thom's 'catastrophe theory' endeavored to map those situations in which gradually changing imbalances culminate in abrupt systemic failure. Among its nonscientific uses, the theory aimed at explaining why relatively smooth changes in stock markets often lead to sudden crashes, why minor disturbances among quiescent populations unexpectedly explode into major social upheavals, or why the Soviet Union, which seemed to be surpassing the United States in the 1970s, fell apart in the 1980s. Implicit in Thom's catastrophe theory is the assumption that all systems — biological, mechanical, human — are 'fragile', with the potential for collapse. Thus, while a system might prove capable of enormous expansion and growth, even when sustaining internal crises for extended periods, it can, as Thom explains, suddenly unravel if it fails to adapt to changing circumstances, loses its equilibrium, or develops 'negative feedback loops' compounding existing strains.

For Corvus — or Faye — the liberal collapse, 'the tipping point', looks as if it will occur sometime between 2010 and 2020, when the confluence of several gradually mounting internal failures culminate in something more apocalyptic. Though the actual details and date of the impending collapse are, of course, unpredictable, this, he argues, makes it no less certain. And though its effects will be terrible, resulting in perhaps billions of dead, the chaos and violence it promises will nevertheless prepare the way for a return to more enduring truths.

What is this system threatening collapse and what are the forces provoking it? Simply put, it is the techno-economic system born of

Eighteenth-century liberalism — whose principal exemplar has been the United States and North Atlantic Europe, but whose global impetus now holds the whole world in its grip.

Faye's work does not, however, focus on the system *per se*. There is already a large literature devoted to it and, in several earlier works, he has examined it at length. The emphasis in *Convergence des catastrophes* is on delineating the principal fault lines along which collapse is likely to occur. For the globalization of liberal socioeconomic forms, he argues, now locks all the world's peoples into a single complex planetary system whose fragility increases as it becomes increasingly interdependent. Though it is difficult to isolate the catastrophes threatening it (for they overlap with and feed off one another), he believes they will take the following forms:

1. The cancerization of the social fabric that comes when an aging European population is deprived of its virile, self-confident traditions; when drug use, permissiveness, and family decline become the norm; when a dysfunctional education system no longer transmits the European heritage; when the Culture Industry fosters mass cretinization; when the Third World consolidates its invasion of the European homelands; and, finally, when the enfeebling effects of these tendencies take their toll on all the other realms of declining European life.

2. The worsening social conditions accompanying these tendencies, he predicts, will be exacerbated by an economic crisis (or crises) born of massive indebtedness, speculation, non-regulation, corruption, interdependence, and financial malpractices whose global ramifications promise a 'correction' more extreme than that of the 1930s.

3. These social and economic upheavals are likely to be compounded by ecological devastation and radical climatic shifts that accelerate deforestation and desiccation, disrupt food supplies, spread famine and disease, deplete natural resources (oil, along with land and water), and highlight the unsustainability of the world's present overpopulation.

4. The scarcity and disorders these man-made disasters bring will not only provoke violent conflicts, but cause the already discredited state to experience increased paralysis, enhancing thus

the prospect of global chaos, especially as it takes the form of strife between a cosmopolitan North and an Islamic South.

These catastrophes, Faye argues, are rooted in practices native to liberal modernity. For the globalization of Western civilizational forms, particularly American-style consumerism, has created a latently chaotic situation, given that its hyper-technological, interconnected world system, dependent on international trade, driven by speculators, and indifferent to virtually every non-economic consideration, is vulnerable to a diverse range of malfunctions. Its pathological effects have indeed already begun to reach their physical limit. For once the billion-plus populations of India and China, already well embarked on the industrializing process, start mass-producing cars, the system will become increasingly unsustainable. The resource depletion and environmental degradation that will follow, though, are only one of the system's tipping points.

No less serious, the globalizing process creates a situation in which minor, local disputes assume planetary significance, as conflicts in remote parts of the world are imposed on the more advanced parts, and vice versa. ('The 9/11 killers were over here', Pat Buchanan writes, 'because we were over there'.) In effect, America's 'Empire of Disorder' is no longer restricted to the periphery, but now threatens the metropolis. Each new advance in globalization accordingly tends to diminish the frontier between external and internal wars, just as American-sponsored globalization provokes the terrorism it ostensibly resists. The cascading implication of these developments have, in fact, become more evident. For instance, if one of the hijacked Boeings of 9/11 had not been shot down over Pennsylvania and instead reached Three Mile Island, the entire Washington-New York area would have been turned into a mega-Chernobyl—destroying the U.S. economy, as well as the global order dependent on it. A miniature nuke smuggled into an East Coast port by any of the ethnic gangs specializing in illegal shipments would have a similar effect. Revealingly, speculation on such doomsday scenarios is now treated as fully plausible.

But even barring a dramatic act of violence, catastrophe looms in all the system's domains, for it is as much threatened by its own entropy (in the form of social-racial disorder, economic crisis, and ecological degradation), as it is by more frontal assaults. This is especially the case with the global economy, whose short-term casino mentality refuses the slightest accountability. Accordingly, its movers and shakers think nothing of casting their fate to fickle stock markets, running up bankrupting debts, issuing fiat credit, fostering a materialistic culture of unbridled consumption, undermining industrial values, encouraging outsourcing, deindustrialization, and wage cutting, just as they remain impervious to the ethnocidal effects of international labor markets and the growing criminality of corporate practices.

Such irresponsible behaviors are, in fact, simply another symptom of the impending crisis, for the system's thinkers and leaders are no longer able to distinguish between reality and their 'virtualist' representation of it, let alone acknowledge the folly of their practices. Obsessed with promoting the power and privileges sustaining their crassly materialist way of life and the progressive, egalitarian, and multicultural principles undergirding the global market, they see the world only in ways they are programmed to see it. The ensuing 'reality gap' deprives them, then, of the capacity both to adapt to changing circumstances or address the problems threatening the system's operability. (The way the Bush White House gathers and interprets 'intelligence', accepting only that which accords with its ideological criteria, is perhaps the best example of this.) In such a spirit, the system's leaders tirelessly assure us that everything is getting better, that new techniques will overcome the problems generated by technology, that unbridled materialism and self-gratification have no costs, that cultural nihilism is a form of liberation, that the problems caused by climatic changes, environmental degradation, overpopulation, and shrinking energy reserves will be solved by extending and augmenting the practices responsible for them. These dysfunctional practices are indeed pursued as if they are crucial to the system's self-legitimacy. Thus, at the very moment when the system's self-corrective mechanisms have been marginalized and the downhill slide has become increasingly immune to correction, the charlatans, schemers, and careerists in charge persist in propagating the belief that everything is 'hunky-dory'.

Karl Marx spilled a great deal of ink lambasting ideologues who thought capitalism arose from natural principles, that all hitherto existing societies had preordained the market's triumph, or that a social order subordinate to economic imperatives represented the highest stage of human achievement. Today, the 'new global bourgeoisie' gives its Euro-nationalist critics even greater cause for ridicule.

Paralyzed by an ideology that bathes itself in optimistic bromides, the system's rulers 'see nothing and understand nothing', assuming that the existing order, in guaranteeing their careers, is a paragon of civilizational achievement, that the 20,000 automobiles firebombed every year in France by Muslim gangs is not a sign of impending race war, that the non-white hordes ethnically cleansing European neighborhoods will eventually be turned into peaceful, productive citizens, that the Middle East will democratize, that the spread of human rights, free markets, and new technologies will culminate in a consumer paradise, that limitless consumption is possible and desirable, that everyone, in effect, can have it all.

Nothing, Faye argues, can halt the system's advance toward the abyss. The point of no return has, indeed, already been passed. Fifteen years of above average temperatures, rising greenhouse gases, melting ice caps, conspicuous ecological deterioration, and the imminent peaking of oil reserves, combined with an uncontrolled Third World demographic boom, massive First World indebtedness, social policies undermining the state's monopoly on our loyalties, and a dangerous geopolitical realignment — each of these potentially catastrophic developments is preparing the basis of the impending collapse. Those who think a last minute international agreement will somehow save the day simply whistle pass the graveyard. Washington's attitude (even more pig-headed than Beijing's) to the modest Kyoto Accords — which would have slowed down, not halted greenhouse emissions — is just one of the many signs that the infernal machine cannot be halted. The existing states and international organizations are, in any case, powerless to do anything, especially the sclerotic 'democracies' of Europe and United States, for their corrupt, short-sighted leaders have not the slightest understanding of what is happening under their very noses, let alone the will to take decisive action against it. Besides, they would rather subsidize bilingual education and Gay Pride parades (or, on the conservative side, ban Darwin) than carry out structural reforms that might address some of their more glaring failures. For such a system, the sole solution, Faye insists, is collapse.

The ecological, economic, demographic, social, civilizational, and geopolitical cataclysms now gradually in the process of converging will eventually bring about the collapse of liberalism's techno-economic civilization. In one of the most striking parts of his book, Faye juxtaposes two very different TV images to illustrate the nature of the present predicament: one is of a troubled President Bush, whose Forrest Gump antics left him noticeably perplexed on 9/11; the other is of the traditionally-dressed, but Kalashnikov-bearing bin Laden, posing as a new Mohammed, calmly and confidently proclaiming the inevitable victory of his ragtag jihadists. These two images — symbolizing the archaic violence that promises to disturb the narcoticized sleep of a decaying modernity — sum up for Faye the kind of world in which we live, especially in suggesting that the future belongs to militant traditionalists rooted in their ancestral heritage, rather than high-tech, neo-liberal 'wimps' like Bush, unconscious of 'the best which has been thought and said in the world'.

In rejecting liberalism's monstrous perversion of European life, Faye does so not as a New Age Luddite or a Left-wing environmentalist. He argues that a techno-economic civilization based on universalist and egalitarian principles is a loathsome abnormality — destructive of future generations and past accomplishments. Rejecting its often technological, bureaucratic, cosmopolitan, and anti-white practices, he fully accepts modern science. He simply states the obvious: Europe's great technological and economic accomplishments cannot be extended to the world's six billion people — let alone tomorrow's ten billion — without fatal consequence. For this reason, he predicts that science and industry in a post-catastrophe world will have no choice but to change, becoming the province of a small elite, not the liberal farce that attempts to transform all the world's peoples into American-style consumers. Similarly, Faye proposes no restoration of lost forms, but rather the revitalization of those ancient spirits, which might enable Europeans to engage the future with the confidence and daring of their ancestors. Thus, as befits a work of prophecy, Faye's survey of the impending tempests aims at preparing his people for what is to come, when the high flood waters and hurricane winds clear away the system's ethnocidal illusions and create the occasion for another self-assertion of European being. It aims, in a word, at helping Europeans resume the epic of their destiny.

National Vanguard, May 29, 2005

4

TEN UNTIMELY IDEAS

The struggle Europeans wage for the genetic, cultural, and territorial heritage of their people is no less a struggle for those ideas necessary to their survival.

Here, freely translated from Guillaume Faye's *Pourquoi nous combattons* (2001) and *L'Archéofuturisme* (1998), are ten ideas I think relevant to this struggle.

1. EUROPE is at war, but doesn't know it . . . It is occupied and colonized by peoples from the Global South and economically, strategically, and culturally subjugated by America's New World Order . . . It is the sick man of the world. (*Pourquoi*, page 9.)

2. ARCHEOFUTURISM: The spirit in which the future arises from a resurgence of ancestral values, as notions of modernity and traditionalism are dialectically overcome . . . To confront the future, especially today, dictates a recourse to an archaic mentality that is premodern, inegalitarian, and non-humanistic, a mentality that restores ancestral values and those of social order . . . The future is thus neither the negation of tradition nor that of a people's historical memory, but rather its metamorphosis and ultimately its growth and regeneration. (*L'Archéofuturisme*, 11, 59, 72.)

3. IDENTITY: Characteristic of humanity is the diversity and singularity of its peoples and cultures. Every homogenization is synonymous with death and sclerosis . . . Ethnic identity and cultural identity form a block, but biological identity is primary,

for without it culture and civilization are impossible to sustain
... Identity is never frozen. It remains itself only in evolving,
reconciling being and becoming. (*Pourquoi*, 146-48.)

4. BIOPOLITICS: A political project responsive to a people's biological and demographic imperatives ... Biopolitics is guided by
the principle that a people's biological quality is essential to its
survival and well-being. (*Pourquoi*, 63-64.)

5. SELECTION: The collective process, based on a competition that
minimizes or eliminates the weak and selects out the strong and
capable. Selection entails both the natural evolution of a species and the historical development of a culture and civilization
... Contemporary society prevents a just selection and instead
imposes a savage, unjust one based on the law of the jungle.
(*Pourquoi*, 212-13.)

6. INTERREGNUM: The period between the end of one civilization and the possible birth of another. We are currently living
through an interregnum, a tragic historical moment when everything is in flames and when everything, like a Phoenix, might
rise reborn from its ashes. (*Pourquoi*, 153.)

7. ETHNIC CIVIL WAR: Only the outbreak of such a war will
resolve the problems created by Europe's current colonization,
Africanization, and Islamization ... Only with their backs to
the wall is a people spurred to come up with solutions that in
other times would be unthinkable. (*Pourquoi*, 130.)

8. REVOLUTION: The violent reversal of a political situation that
follows a profound crisis and is the work of an 'active minority' ... A true revolution is a metamorphosis, that is, a radical
reversal of all values. The sole revolutionary of the modern era is
Nietzsche ... and not Marx, who sought simply another form of
bourgeois society ... We have, in any case, long passed the point
of no return, where it is possible to arrest the prevailing decay
with moderate political reforms. (*Pourquoi*, 210-11.)

9. ARISTOCRACY: A true aristocracy embodies its people's essence,
which it serves with courage, disinterest, modesty, taste, sim-
plicity, and stature ... To recreate a new aristocracy is the eternal task of every revolutionary project ... The creation of such

an aristocracy is possible only through war, which is the most merciless of selective forces. (*Pourquoi*, 60-61.)

10. WILL TO POWER: The tendency of all life to perpetuate itself, to ensure its survival, and to enhance its domination, its superiority, and its creative capacities . . . The will to power accepts that life is struggle, an eternal struggle for supremacy, the endless struggle to improve and perfect oneself, the absolute refusal of nihilism, the opposite of contemporary relativism . . . It is the force of life and of history. It is not simply the organic imperative for domination, but for survival and continuity . . . A people or a civilization that abandons its will to power inevitably perishes. (*Pourquoi*, 227.)

National Vanguard, December 18, 2005

5

EUROPE'S ENEMY: ISLAM OR AMERICA?

Apropos of Guillaume Faye, *Le Coup d'État mondial: Essai sur le Nouvel Impérialisme Américain.* Paris: L'Æncre, 2004.

Fas est et ab hoste doceri. (It is permitted to learn from the enemy)
— Ovid

This past spring, for the sixth time in six years, Guillaume Faye has published a book that reshapes the discourse of European nationalism ('nationalism' here referring not to the Nineteenth-century 'nation-state', but to the 'nation' of *Magna Europa*). Like each of his previous works, *Le Coup d'État mondial* addresses the exigencies of the moment, as well as the perennial concerns of the European *ethnos*. In this spirit, it offers a scathing critique of both the 'New American Imperialism' and the European anti-Americanism opposing it, simultaneously contributing to the larger nationalist debate on Europe's destiny.

Framed in terms of Carl Schmitt's *Freund/Feind* designation, this debate centers on the question: who is Europe's enemy? During the Cold War, the more advanced nationalists rejected the official view that Soviet Communism was the principal enemy and instead designated the United States. This is evident in the work of Francis Parker Yockey, Jean Thiriart, Adriano Romualdi, Otto Strasser, and Alain de Benoist, as well in the politics of the sole European statesman to have defended Europe's independence in the postwar period: Charles de Gaulle.

* * *

45

Today, this anti-Americanism persists, but has come to signify something quite different than what it did during the Cold War. What changed, and this starts to be evident in the late 1980s and even more so in the '90s, is Third World immigration, which puts the American threat in an entirely altered perspective. In Euro-nationalist ranks, Faye stands out as the principal proponent of the view that Islam and its non-white immigrants now constitute Europe's enemy and that America, though still an adversary, represents a qualitatively less threatening menace.

Contrary to its apologists' claims, Faye argues that the New American Imperialism (NAI) of the Bush Administration is not the hard-headed, morally-clear assertion of American power that they make of it, but rather a puerile, utopian, and unrealistic one based on the premise that *tout est permis!*—that anything goes. The U.S. may be the world's dominant power, but in Faye's view it lacks what Aristotle and the conservative tradition of statecraft understood as the basis of enduring power: prudence. Its hubristic confusion of dominance with omnipotence is indeed preparing the NAI's neoconservative architects—and America—for a tragic fall.

To assume, though, that the U.S. has not just the right, but the capacity to dominate the planet is nothing, Faye observes, if not simple-minded. The NAI's proponents might think they have broken with the legalistic or Kantian postulates of liberal internationalism by pursuing hegemonist objectives with military methods and a narrowly defined sense of the nation's interests (which, in itself, would be less objectionable), but their readiness to substitute raw power for other forms of power (that is, their readiness to forsake U.S. influence in the 'thieves' den' of the UN or in those international regulatory agencies which the U.S. created after 1945) is informed by a self-serving (and ultimately self-defeating) belief in America's divine mission. Deluding themselves that they do God's work in the world, that their imperial adventures are biblically sanctioned, they cannot but disconnect themselves from the intractable reality they seek to dominate.

Despite its imperialist ambitions, America is not Rome. Faye claims it is more like a house of cards—an ephemeral economic-political enterprise—lacking those ethnic, religious, and cultural traits that go into making a great people and a Great Power. As any white Californian will attest, there is, in fact, no longer anything particularly American about America, only people like the turbaned Sikh who drives the local cab, the Mexican illegal who mows our neighbor's lawn or tars his roof, the Indian programmer who replaces his higher-paid white counterpart, the Chinese grocer who sells us beer and cigarettes late at night, the African who empties the bedpans in our nursing homes, the Africans of American birth who run our cities and public agencies, and, finally, those whites in distant suburbs, refugees from post-American America.

For Faye, this hodgepodge of disparate peoples is not a nation in any historical sense, only a fabricated social system, whose members, as Lewis Lapham writes, are 'united by little else except the possession of a credit card and a password to the internet'. Why, it seems almost unnecessary to ask, would an American Gurkha risk his life for such an entity?

The military technology of Imperial America may lack an equal, but its centrality to U.S. power, Faye argues, testifies to the enfeebled cognitive capacity of its ruling elites, who think their computerized gadgetry can replace those primordial human qualities that go into making a people or a nation — qualities like those that steeled not just Rome's republican legions, but the Celtic-Saxon ranks of the Confederacy, the gunmen of the IRA, the indomitable battalions of the Wehrmacht, and the Red Army of the Great Patriotic War. In the absence of such qualities forged by blood and history, the NAI's space-age military (whose recruiters now slip beneath the border to find the 'volunteers' for its imperial missions) is actually a paper tiger, no match for a nation in arms — not even a pathetic, misbegotten nation like Iraq.

The hubris-ridden neoconservatives who led America into the sinking sands of Mesopotamia did so without the slightest consideration of the toll it would take on the country's already stressed and overtaxed institutions. Fighting for objectives that are everywhere contested and with troops that have no idea of what they are dying for, the only thing they have accomplished in their crusading zeal is what they set out to combat: having inflamed the Middle East, enhanced Islam's prestige, augmented bin Laden's ranks, accelerated the proliferation of weapons of mass destruction, and turned the whole world against them.

Finally, Faye depicts the NAI as America's last bloom. Both domestically and internationally, he claims the signs of American decline are increasingly evident. Its melting pot, for example, no longer assimilates, its mixed-race population is inextricably Balkanized, its state is increasingly dysfunctional (except in its anti-white, anti-family, anti-community practices), and its market, the one remaining basis of social integration, is in serious difficulty, burdened by massive trade imbalances, unable to generate industrial jobs, hampered by astronomical debts and deficits, and increasingly dependent on the rest of the world for loans and investment. Even the country's fabled democracy has ceased to work, with elections decided by the courts, fraudulent polling practices, big money, and the rule of spin and simulacra. The virtuality of the political process seems, in fact, to reflect the illusory authority of its reigning elites, whose oligarchic disposition and incompetent management now necessitates the existing system of smoke and mirrors.

Internationally, American prospects seem no less bleak. Faye points out that the almighty dollar, for 60 years the world's reserve currency, is today threatened (which means the country will eventually no longer be able to live on credit); the European Union and Asia's economic colossus are undermining its primacy in world markets; it faces the wrath of a billion Muslims worldwide and does nothing to stem Muslim immigration to the U.S.; its occupation of Iraq is causing it to hemorrhage monetarily, morally, and militarily; and, not least, its image and integrity have been so blackened that raw power alone prolongs its discredited hegemony.

Unlike the implicit imperialism of the Cold War era, the NAI is openly anti-European. In this vein, it opposes the Continent's political (rather than economic) unification; treats its allies, even its special British poodle, with contempt; practices a divide and rule tactic that pits the so-called New Europe against the Old; and pursues a strategy to contain Europe and keep it dependent on the U.S. security system.

* * *

In parallel with America's anti-Europeanism, there has developed in Europe what Faye calls an 'obsessional and hysterical anti-Americanism' (OHAA). He sees this development as completely self-destructive of Europe's self-interest, suggesting, perhaps tongue-in-cheek, that it may be the CIA's handiwork. For this anti-Americanism bears little relation to earlier forms of French anti-Americanism, which sought to defend France's High Culture from the subversions of America's Culture Industry or else the nation's sovereignty from U.S. efforts to undermine it. Even the Right-wing proponents of OHAA are not firmly within the pale of 'the new revolutionary nationalism', which designates liberalism's cosmopolitan plutocracy as the chief enemy and resists the denationalization of capital, population, and territory. Instead, this OHAA not only does nothing to advance the European project, its fixation on the NAI inadvertently contributes to the Continent's Islamization and Third Worldization, hastening, in effect, its demise as a civilizational force.

Touching the government and numerous nationalist tendencies, in addition to the perennially anti-identitarian Left, this OHAA is informed by a simple-minded manichaeanism which assumes that America's enemy (Islam) is Europe's friend and possible savior. In effect, this sort of anti-Americanism adopts not just the manichaean worldview of Islam, but that of the Judeo-Protestants who make up Bush's political base. For like the neoconservative publicists and propagandists advising the administration and like the mullahs shepherding their submissive, but fanatical flocks, those touched by the OHAA paint the world in black and white terms, the axis of good versus the axis of evil, with the enemy (America or Islam) taken as the source of all evil and their side (America or Islam) as the seat of all virtue.

And just as the liberal/neocon image of America is Hebraic, not Greco-European, these European anti-Americans carry in their demonstrations the flags of Iraq, Palestine, Algeria, and Morocco, chant 'Allahu Akbar', and affirm their solidarity with Islam — all without the slightest affirmation of Europe's own people and culture. Worse, the politicians catering to this anti-Americanism oppose U.S. policies less for the sake of Europe's autonomy than for that of its ever-growing Muslim minority. They thus refuse to be an American protectorate, at the very moment they risk becoming an Islamic-Arabic colony (Eurabia). More disturbing still, the OHAA's identity-confusing manichaeanism influences not just left-wing organizations bent on subverting Europe's bioculture and New Class politicians driven by globalist imperatives, but also French New Rightists around Alain de Benoist, revolutionary nationalists around Christian Bouchet, Evolean traditionalists around the Austrian Martin Schwartz and the Italian Claudio Mutti, various Eurasianists, as well as many lesser known tendencies, all of whom mistake their simple-minded anti-Americanism with resistance to liberalism's cosmopolitan plutocracy.

Though Faye stresses that the economic and cultural war the U.S. wages on Europe warrants the firmest of European ripostes, for its alleged defenders to feel the slightest solidarity with Islam, even when 'unjustly' attacked, is simply masochistic — for, if the last 1,400 years is any guide, Islam seeks nothing so much as to conquer and destroy Europe. America's plutocratic liberalism may be responsible for fostering transnational labor markets that import millions of Third World immigrants into the white homelands, but if the latter are ignored for the sake of resisting the former, the end result may soon be the extinction of Europe's bioculture. (Medically, this would be equivalent to fighting typhoid by concentrating exclusively on the contaminated food and water transmitting it, while neglecting the infectious bacillus assaulting the sufferer — in which case the disease might be contained, but at the cost of the patient's life.)

This sort of anti-Americanism, Faye surmises, ends up not just misconceiving Europe's enemy, but sanctioning its colonization, including the colonization of its mind. For in the same way the 'poor African' is seen as 'victimized' by white colonialism, Europe for the OHAA is seen as a victim of U.S. imperialism. And we know from experiences on our side of the Atlantic that such a mentality takes responsibility for nothing and attributes everything it finds objectionable to the white man, in this case the American.

More pathetically still, in designating the U.S. as an enemy and Islam as a friend, these anti-Americans inadvertently dance to Washington's own tune. Based on his *La Colonisation de l'Europe: Discours vrai sur l'immigration et l'Islam* (2000) and in reference to Alexandre Del Valle's *Islamisme et États-Unis: Une alliance contre l'Europe* (1999), Faye contends that since the early 1980s U.S. policy has aggressively promoted Europe's Third Worldization: through its ideology of human rights, multiculturalism, and multiracialism, through its unrelenting efforts to force the European Union to admit Muslim Turkey, but above all through its intervention on behalf of Islam in the Yugoslavian civil war. In all these ways fostering social, religious, cultural, and ethnic divisions which neutralize Europe's potential threat to its own hegemony, the U.S. has sought to subvert European unity.

Faye suggests that this anti-American neurosis, like a classic textbook pathology, designates the U.S. as its enemy for fear of acknowledging the danger looming under its very nose. In this spirit, anti-American Islamophiles refuse to see what's happening in their own lands, whose soft, dispirited white population is increasingly cowed by Islam's conquering life force. For however much American policy assaults Europe, the danger it poses is qualitatively less threatening than the prospect of Islamic colonization. To think otherwise, he argues is possible only by ignoring the primacy of race and culture.

Instead, then, of pursuing chimerical relations with people whose underlying motive is the destruction of Europe, it would be wiser for Europeans to view what's happening in Iraq as the Chinese and Indians do: with cynical detachment and an eye to their own self-interest.

* * *

The greatest danger to Europe, and this idea is the axis around which Faye's argument revolves, comes from the Islamic lands to the 'South', whose non-white immigrants are presently colonizing the Continent, assuming control of its biosphere, and altering the foundations of European life. For European nationalists and governments to treat America, with its shallow, provisional power, as the enemy and Islam, with its non-white multitudes pressing on Europe's borders, as its friend is the height of folly, for it ignores the fundamental polarity separating the peoples of the North from those of the South.

Not coincidentally, this sort of anti-Americanism mimics the anti-white sensibility found in American liberal and neoconservative ranks. For like those who try to convince us that America is a 'creed', not a white Christian nation, these anti-Americans allying with Islam to fight the 'ricains' betray their *patrie* — treating it as an abstraction and not a people. If Americans, then, would do better using their troops to defend their porous borders, instead of playing cowboy in Mesopotamia, Europeans loyal to their heritage would do better to resist, rather than to make common cause with those who are presently invading their homeland.

Faye's *Coup d'État mondial* offers, thus, a powerful antidote to the anti-Americans' false and potentially fatal reasoning. At the same time, it demystifies the new American imperialism, revealing its tenuous character; it exposes the self-destructive character of an opposition refusing to recognize Europe's real enemy; and, most important, in designating the enemy — the non-white colonizers who hope to turn Europe into a *Dar-al-Islam* — it designates what is the single, most unavoidable, and absolutely necessary duty of European peoples everywhere: the defense of their children, their homeland, and their future.

The Occidental Quarterly 5, no. 3 (Fall 2005)

6

FROM DUSK TO DAWN: GUILLAUME FAYE SPEAKS IN MOSCOW

TRANSLATOR'S NOTE: *The following talk was given in Moscow on May 17, 2005, and recently posted, in French, on the Russian site Athenaeum.*

For at least three reasons, it deserves the widest circulation in ethnonationalist circles. The first is one which more and more English-speaking nationalists are beginning to realize: Guillaume Faye today is the most interesting, if not pertinent spokesman for the genetic-cultural heritage associated with European America. Everything he says or writes on the subject of who we are, what we are fighting for, and where the main battlefronts will lie are worth thinking about. In France, Belgium, the Netherlands, Spain, Portugal, Italy, and now Russia, his ideas have touched the leading debates.

The second reason I think this article deserves attention is metapolitical. Faye is a veteran of the first major effort to practice a 'Gramscianism of the Right'—that is, to wage a cultural war against the ethnocidal principles of the dominant liberal culture. Not unrelatedly, he stands out among anti-liberal nationalists, creative force that he is, in having developed a language and a discourse that reaches beyond the narrow limits of sectarians and marginals, while offering a radical alternative to the anti-white discourse of the existing system.

The third reason is that this talk is a succinct and eloquent synthesis of the ideas — the vision — Faye has developed in the seven books (and countless articles) he's produced in the eight years since the appearance of his path-breaking L'Archéofuturisme (1998). However provisionally

53

sketched, these ideas aim at helping us through what promises to be the worst storm of our collective existence. At the same time, they speak to something more primordial.

An earlier student of our historical destiny contends: 'All that is great stands in the storm' (Plato). What is coming will undoubtedly determine if we have any greatness left in us. 'The white men of the West', the men of the Evening Lands (Abendländer), having gone under before, have a long history of resolutely confronting the dangers bearing down on and, in doing so, of rediscovering what is still great within themselves.

Faye, I believe, is calling us to return to ourselves, as we turn to face what is coming — M.O.

Not since the fall of the Roman Empire has Europe experienced such a dramatic situation. It faces a danger unparalleled in its history and doesn't even know it — or rather refuses to see it.

It's been invaded, occupied, and colonized by peoples from the South and by Islam. It's dominated by the United States, which wages a merciless economic war on it. It's collapsing demographically, as its population ages and it ceases to reproduce itself. It's been emasculated by decadent, nihilist ideologies cloaked in a facile optimism, and it's been subjected to an unprecedented regression of culture and education, to primitivism and materialism. Europe is the sick man of the world. And its political classes, along with its intellectual elites, are actively collaborating in this race suicide. The argument I'm making is not, though, just about immigration, but also about a colonization and an invasion that is transforming Europe's biological and ethno-cultural stock; it's about not giving way to despair; about seeing that the struggle is only just beginning; and knowing that Europe's closely related peoples have no alternative but to unite in their common defense.

The Destruction of Europe's Ethno-Biological Stock

The demographics of the non-white invasion of France and Europe are terrifying. In a recent work, *La France africaine* (African France), a well-known demographer predicts that if present trends continue, more than 40 percent of the French population will be Black or Arab by 2040. Twenty-five percent of schoolchildren in France and Belgium today and more than 30 percent of infants are already of non-European origin. Of France's present population of 61 million, more than 10 million are non-European and have a far higher birth rate than the native French. Every year 100,000 non-Europeans are naturalized as French citizens and another 300,000, most illegal, cross our undefended borders. The situation is not much different throughout the rest of Europe and signals the virtual end of our civilization, though the political classes have apparently yet to notice it.

Worldwide, including the United States, the European race is in steep numerical decline. It's often said that our technological superiority will compensate for this disparity, but I don't think so: the only meaningful forms of wealth and power are in human beings. For a civilization is based primarily on what the Romans called *germen*, that is, the ethno-biological stock, the roots, that nourish a civilization and culture.

The non-European invasion of Europe that began in the 1960s was largely self-engendered, provoked by Left and Right-wing politicians contaminated with Marxist and Trotskyist ideas; by an employer class greedy for cheap labor; by Jewish intellectuals demanding a multiracial society; and by the ideology of human rights that has sprung from the secularization of certain Christian principles.

In France and in Europe, the collaborators abetting the invasion have established a system of preferences for the invaders that native whites are obliged to support. Illegal immigrants are thus not only rarely repatriated when caught, they continue to receive the lavish social welfare benefits handed out to them by the liberal elites controlling the state. At the same time, 'anti-racists' have introduced a host of discriminatory laws that protect immigrants from normal social restraints, even though they are largely responsible for the ongoing explosion of criminality (more than 1,000 percent in the last 50 years).

The invasion is taking place as much in the maternity wards as it is along our porous borders. Combined with the demographic decline of the white population, immigration has become an economic disaster for Western Europe. It's estimated to cost $180 billion per year (if the growing insecurity, as well as the innumerable forms of social assistance benefiting immigrants, including illegals, is figured in). This, in turn, creates new attractions for the invaders: it is simply far more 'interesting' to be unemployed in Europe than to work in the Third World. While the educated and creative segments of our population are beginning to flee, mainly to the United States, they are being replaced by Africa's refuse, which has to be fed and supported by us and hasn't anything in the way of skills or intelligence to offer in return.

All these facts suggest that the Twenty-first-century European economy will be a depressed, Third World one.

Islam's Third Major Offensive

In addition to this mass, non-white invasion, Islam is again on the offensive. With single-minded persistence, its totalitarian and aggressive religion/ideology seeks the conquest of Europe. We've already suffered three great assaults by Islam, whose lands stretch from Gibraltar to Indonesia. The first of these offensives was halted at Poitiers in 732 by Charles Martel; the second in 1683, during the Ottoman siege of Vienna; the third [in the form of the present invasion and colonization] is now underway [and virtually unopposed]. Islam has a long memory and its objective is to establish on our Continent what [the leader of Iran's Islamic Revolution, Ayatollah) Khomeini called the 'universal Caliphate'.

The invasion of Europe is underway and the figures [testifying to its extent] are alarming. The Continent, including Russia, is now occupied by 55 million Muslims, a number that increases at a 6 percent annual rate. In France, there are at least 6 million. Like those in Belgium and Britain, these French Muslims are starting to demand a share of political power. The government, for its part, simply refuses to take seriously their objective of transforming France into an Islamic Republic by the year 2020, when the demographic weight of the Arab/Muslim population will have become determinant. Meanwhile, the government continues to finance the construction of mosques throughout the country in the hope of buying social peace; there are already more than 2,000 in France, nearly double the number in Morocco. Islam is at present the second largest religion in France, behind Catholicism, but the largest in the numbers of practitioners. [The republic's president] Jacques Chirac has even declared that 'France is now an Islamic power'. Everywhere in the West there prevails the unfounded belief that there's a difference between Islam and 'Islamism', and that a Western, secularized, that is, moderate

Islam, is possible. There's no such thing. Every Muslim is potentially a jihadist. For Islam is a theocracy that confuses the spiritual with the temporal, faith with law, and seeks to impose its *shari'a* [Islamic law] on a Europe whose civilizational precepts are absolutely incompatible with it.

The Impending Race War

Criminality and delinquency in Western Europe, caused by mass immigration and the collapse of civic values, have now reached intolerable levels. In France in 2004, tens of thousands of cars were torched and 80 policemen killed by Afro-Arab gangs. Nearly every week race riots erupt in the *banlieues* [the 'suburbs' housing the immigrant masses]. In the public schools, violence is endemic and educational levels have almost collapsed. Among youth under 20, nearly 20 percent are illiterate. While racist assaults on whites are steadily rising, they are routinely ignored by the media in the name of the anti-racist vulgate, which holds that only whites can be racists. At the same time, an arsenal of repressive legislation, worthy of Soviet Communism, has imposed 'laws' whose purely ideological and subjective intent make no pretence to fairness, let alone objectivity. All criticism of immigration or Islam is legally prohibited. I myself have been prosecuted several times and levied with an enormous fine for having written *La Colonisation de l'Europe* [The Colonization of Europe].

A race war is foreseeable now in several European countries, a subterranean war that will be far more destructive than 'terrorism'. The white population is already being displaced, a sort of genocide is being carried out against it with the complicity or the abstention of the ruling class, the media, and the politicians, for the ideology of these collaborating elites is infused with a pathological hatred of their own people and a morbid passion for miscegenation.

The state's utopian plan for 'republican integration' has nevertheless failed because it thought peaceful coexistence between foreigners and natives, non-whites and whites, was possible in a single territory. Our rulers haven't read Aristotle, who taught that no City can possibly be democratic and orderly if it isn't ethnically homogeneous . . . European societies today are devolving into an unmanageable ethnic chaos.

I'm a native of Southwest France, of the area along the Atlantic coast, and speak not a word of Russian, but I feel infinitely closer to a Russian than to a French-speaking Arab or African, even if they happen to be 'French' citizens.

The Moral Crisis and Archeofuturism

The present situation can be explained, almost clinically, as a form of 'mental AIDS'. These afflictions are spread by the virus of nihilism, which Nietzsche foresaw, and which has weakened all our natural defenses. Thus infected, Europeans have succumbed to a mania for self-extinction, having voluntarily opened the city gates to the invaders.

The first symptom of this disease is 'xenophilia': a systematic preference for the Other rather than for the Same. A second symptom is 'ethnomasochism', a hatred of one's own civilization and origins. A third is emasculation [dévirilisation], or what might be called the cult of weakness and a preference for male homosexuality. Historically proven values associated with the use of force and a people's survival — values associated with honor, loyalty, family, fertility, patriotism, the will to survive, etc. — are treated today as ridiculous shortcomings. Such decadence owes a good deal to the secularization of Christian charity and its egalitarian offshoot, human rights.

Europeans may take inspiration from certain values still upheld in Russia: for example, the consciousness of belonging to a superior civilization and of maintaining a 'right to distance' from other peoples. We need to break with all forms of 'ethnopluralism', which is simply another kind of egalitarianism, and reclaim the right to 'ethnocentrism', the right to live in our own lands without the Other. We also have to reclaim the principle: 'To each his own'. Besides, only Westerners believe race-mixing is a virtue or envisage the future as a melting pot. They alone believe in cosmopolitanism. The Twenty-first century, though, will be dominated by a resurgence of ethno-religious blocs, especially in the South and the East. Francis Fukuyama's 'end of history' will never happen. Instead, we're going to experience an acceleration of history with the 'clash of civilizations'. Europeans will need, then, to break with the 'presentism' in which they are sunk and learn to see themselves again (as do Muslims, Chinese, and Indians) as a 'long-living people', bearers of a future. The mental revolution needed to bring about this change in European attitudes is, though, only possible through a gigantic crisis, a violent shock, which is already on its way and which I will say a few words about below.

The New American Imperialism

Europeans also have to come to terms with what I called in my last book the 'new American imperialism', an imperialism more heavy-handed than that of the Cold War era, but one that is also more blundering. Since the collapse of the Soviet Union, American administrations seem to have lost all sense of measure, becoming ever more hubristic, as they embark on a fantastic quest for world domination, dressed up in the simulacra of a new Roman empire. Much of this, of course, is explainable in terms of neoconservative ideology, linked with Zionism, but it's also driven by a messianic, almost pathological, sense of having a 'divine mission'.

What are the goals of this new American imperialism? To encircle and neutralize Russia, preventing any meaningful alliance between her and Europe (the Pentagon's worse nightmare); to deflect Europe's challenge to its hegemony by making Islam and Muslim Turkey a part of it; to subjugate the Eastern and Central European parts of the former Soviet empire; to wage a relentless economic war on the European Union and do so in such a way that the latter doesn't dream of resisting. The crusading spirit of this new American imperialism everywhere endeavors to impose its tyrannical system of 'democracy', especially on Russia's periphery. 'Democracy' has actually come to mean 'pro-American regime'.

But we shouldn't complain of these American ambitions, which accord with their state's geopolitical and thalassocratic desire for domination. In history, everyone is responsible only for themselves.

That's why I oppose the 'obsessional and hysterical anti-Americanism' so prevalent in France, for it is counterproductive, self-victimizing, and irresponsible.

A people or nation must learn to distinguish between its 'principal adversary' and its 'principal enemy'. The first tries to dominate and undermine, the second to kill. We shouldn't forget Carl Schmitt's formula: 'It's not only you who chooses your enemy, it's more often your enemy who chooses you'. America, specifically its ruling class, is Europe's and Russia's 'principal adversary' at the level of geopolitics, economics, and culture. Europe's 'principal enemy' is the peoples of the South, increasingly assembled under the banner of Islam, whose invasion of the Continent is already well underway, facilitated by a political class and an intelligentsia who have opened the gates and who seek a miscegenated, non-European Europe (to Washington's delight).

Like Atlanticists, the hysterical anti-Americans overestimate the United States, without understanding that it is only as strong as we are weak. The Americans' catastrophic and counterproductive occupation of Iraq, to which they have brought nothing but chaos, makes this all indisputably evident. In the Twenty-first century, the U.S. will cease to be the premier world power. That will be China — or, if we have the will, what I call 'Euro-Siberia' — a federated alliance between the peoples of the European peninsular and Russia.

The Convergence of Catastrophes

I've postulated the hypothesis that the present global system, founded on a belief in miracles, a belief in indefinite progress, is on the verge of collapse. For the first time in history, humanity as a whole is threatened by a cataclysmic crisis that is likely to occur sometime between 2010 and 2020 — a crisis provoked by the ongoing degradation of the ecosystem and climatic disruptions, by the exhaustion of fossil fuel sources and food-producing capacity, by the increased fragility of an international economic order based on speculation and massive indebtedness, by the return of epidemics, by the rise of nationalism, terrorism, and nuclear proliferation, by the growing aggressiveness of Islam's world offense, and by the dramatic aging of the West's population.

We need to prepare for these converging catastrophes, which will mark the transition from one era to another, as their cataclysmic effects sweep away liberal modernity and bring about a New Middle Age. With such a convergence, there will also come an opportunity for rebirth, for historical regeneration occurs only when challenged by the forces of chaos. This is especially the case with a civilization like our own, whose very nature is 'metamorphic'.

Euro-Siberia

The Europe of the future must no longer be envisaged in the mushy, ungovernable forms of the present European Union, which is a power-less Medusa, unable to control its borders, dominated as it is by the mania of free trade, and subject to American domination. We need to imagine a federal, imperial *Grande Europe*, ethnically homogeneous (that is, European), based on a single autonomous area, and allied to Russia. I call this enormous continental bloc 'Euro-Siberia'. Having no need to be aggressive toward its neighbors because it would be unassailable, such a bloc would become the premier world power (in a world partitioned into large blocs), self-centered, and opposed to all the dangerous dogmas now associated with globalism. It would have the capacity to practice the 'autarky of great spaces', whose principles have already been worked out by the Nobel Prize-winning economist, Maurice Allais. The destiny of the European is indeed now linked to Russia, for both ethno-cultural and geopolitical reasons. It's abso-lutely imperative for America's mercantile thalassocracy to prevent the birth of a Euro-Siberian federation.

This is not the place to speak of the Israeli state. Only a word: for essentially demographic reasons, I believe the Zionist utopia con-ceived by Herzl and Buber and realized after 1948 will not survive any longer than Soviet communism did; indeed, its end is already in sight. I'm presently writing a book on *The New Jewish Question*, which I hope will be translated into Russian.

Conclusion

Fatalism is never appropriate. History is always open-ended and pre-sents innumerable unexpected caprices and turns. Let's not forget the formula of William of Orange: 'Where there's a will, there's a way'. The period we are presently living through is a one of resistance and of preparation for the even more threatening events to come, such as might follow the juncture of a race war and a massive economic downturn. We need to start thinking in post-chaos terms and organize accordingly.

In closing, let me leave you with a favorite watchword of mine: 'From Resistance to Reconquest, From Reconquest to Renaissance'.

National Vanguard, February 27, 2006

French original: 'Du crépuscule à l'aube',
http://www.ateney.ru/frans/fr001.htm

7

THE THIRD WORLD WAR IS ABOUT TO BEGIN: AN INTERVIEW WITH GUILLAUME FAYE

TRANSLATOR'S NOTE: *The following interviewed appeared in the December issue of the popular Flemish monthly* Menzo. *It was then translated into French and appeared on January 7 at AMI Belgique (the best, in my opinion, of the 19 national editions of the Altermedia News websites). As the geostrategist Robert Steuckers (himself a son of Brave Flanders) notes, this interview is a real coup for Faye, testament to the growing recognition of his prophetic warnings, as well as to the rapidly evolving contours of the European discourse on Islam. In Faye's Paris, by contrast, he has become something of an outlaw. After the publication of his* La Colonisation de l'Europe *in 2000, the government fined him 300,000 francs and imposed a year's suspended sentence on him for 'telling the truth' about Islam — or for what it called 'inciting racial hatred'. The Left-multiculturalist Establishment has been no less unrelenting in denouncing him as a 'racist' and 'fascist' and in keeping him out of the public sphere. His unorthodox opinions have also aroused the hostility (or jealousy) of those 'Right-wing' intellectuals (among them Alain de Benoist), who prefer the elegant cafés of the Boulevard Saint-Germain-des-Prés to the ugly realities facing France's petit blancs. As Machiavelli put it, 'there is nothing more difficult to take in hand, more perilous to conduct, or more uncertain in its success, than to take the lead in the introduction of a new order of things'. It is, however, becoming increasingly difficult to stigmatize or marginalize this irrepressible Cassandra, who has done so much to awaken Europe to the dangers threatening it. This is evident not only in the fact that a mass-circulation magazine like* Menzo *(with a readership estimated at a half-million) should interview him, but also that the Russian Duma recently honored him for his work and that later this year an international conference on 'the future of the white race' will be held in Moscow under his auspices. Though the following interview reflects the constraints in language and concept that the mainstream media imposes, enough of Faye's ideas come through, I hope, to interest our readership. Slight cuts in the text are indicated by ellipses (. . .) and the translator's additions by brackets. — M.O.*

Menzo: Do you really believe this scenario [sketched in your *Avant-Guerre* predicting a race war of world-historical proportions in the white West]?

Guillaume Faye: I do — just as much as I believe that if you drive down the wrong side of the freeway you will eventually have a head-on collision. The precise moment such a collision will occur is difficult to predict, but it is certainly bound to happen. Within ten years or so we are going to be confronted with something never before seen. But more than race war, we are going to experience economic breakdowns, ecological crises, and catastrophic shortages of oil. . . . All the world's governments operate with short-term agendas and nothing at this point is more disastrous. It is often said that the Earth is sick. But it is man that is sick.

Menzo: Following the assault on the Twin Towers, we have become increasingly conscious of how vulnerable the global economy is. What possible alternative is there to it?

Guillaume Faye: Globalization was born not in the last decade, but in the Sixteenth century. This fact, however, is not going to avert the impending catastrophe [it is fostering]. An alternative to it is what I call *l'autarchie économique des grands espaces* [that is, a *Großraum* or continental autarky]. In continental areas, like Europe, there would be free circulation of goods, capital, and labor [but barriers raised against other geo-economic blocs]. If all the great continental spaces, such as Europe, Asia, Africa, etc., practiced such autarkic policies, it would be possible to maintain a certain level of well-being across the globe.

It isn't necessary to sacrifice everything to free trade. The fact that textiles are massively produced in China today has had a terrible effect on the French textile sector. Clothing, however, hasn't gotten cheaper in France nor have Chinese textile workers experienced much of an improvement in their living standards. Only commerce has profited.

Menzo: What importance do you attribute to the global economy?

Guillaume Faye: As much as I attribute to the impossibility of integrating large numbers of immigrants. General de Gaulle used to say: 'In order to make kir [a French cocktail], you need white wine and cassis liqueur. If you add too much cassis, it's no longer kir'. This is another way of saying that it's only possible to integrate a limited number of foreigners. At present, in Seine-Saint-Denis and in certain other departments of the Paris Region (and also in Roubaix and in a number of other French cities), a majority of the population is no longer of French origin. It's impossible to integrate such populations. Economically, the situation is even worse. Out of every hundred [Third World] immigrants who enter Europe, only five enter the workforce. By contrast, one out of every two French university graduates (and the same is true in Belgium) wants to emigrate. This is eventually going to bring down the existing welfare state, which, in turn, will only increase the potential for conflict. The riots we recently experienced [i.e., the 21 nights of riotous anarchy that occurred in November 2005 in the occupied suburbs] are only the prelude to the catastrophe which I expect to begin sometime after 2010. Canada's Wright Foundation is also predicting that in the period 2007-2010, there is going to be another major outbreak of ethnic violence in France. It makes this prediction on the basis of a diverse range of statistics, such as increased levels of violence and crime. Islam's massive concentration in our cities and suburbs is a problem that will soon make itself felt.

Menzo: The riots in November did not, however, have a religious character. The most common explanation for them has been social exclusion and discrimination.

Guillaume Faye: We're always looking for social-economic explanations. This is not only the Marxist way of thinking about conflict, it is

an incorrect way. Immigrants today are receiving massive state supports. I would even argue that illegal immigrants now get better medical care than French natives. Portuguese and Spanish immigrants
who came to France in the 1930s and '40s received no aid at all, but it
was never cause for riot and mayhem. Professor Loland, recipient of
France's Economics Prize and the leading authority on the subject,
estimates that the direct and indirect costs of immigration today is
36 billion euros [$44 billion] a year. This constitutes 80 percent of the
French state's deficit, or 13.5 percent of its annual social security costs.
And this is not Le Pen arguing the point, but a reputable academic.
Every immigrant who crosses our border ends up costing us 100,000
euros. It's absurd, then, to claim that immigrants are neglected. Just
the contrary is true. Clichy-sous-Bois, where the November riots
broke out, receives half of all aid allotted to troubled urban areas. It's
my belief that the instigators of the riots were simply waiting for an
opportunity to riot . . .

Menzo: Is there anything to suggest that organized crime had a role in
instigating the riots? Eighty percent of the rioters [arrested] had some
sort of criminal record.

Guillaume Faye: This is not the way I see it. The riots weren't provoked by Sarkozy [who called them 'scum']. And actually it was only
8 percent of the arrested rioters who had criminal records. . . . In my
view, it was more an [ethnic] revolt than a criminal attack on the
police. It's thus necessary to know why they revolted.

Menzo: Another indication that the riots were the work of criminal
gangs was that the fatwa [Islamic religious injunction] issued by the
Union des organizations islamiques de France [the largest French
Muslim association] had no effect on the rioters. This suggests that
the rioters' inspiration wasn't religious.

Guillaume Faye: It is often forgotten that Islam is deceptive on principle. The Koran says that it is perfectly permissible to lie in certain
circumstances, whenever, for example, one is in a weakened state or
whenever it would serve Islam's interests to do so. It is perfectly reasonable, then, to think that Muslims wanted to appear to non-Mus-
lims as opposed to the riots, while amongst themselves they supported

it. Dominique de Villepin [the Prime Minister] has said as much. Of course, this isn't the case with all imams [Muslim leaders or clerics], but it is probably the case with those who see themselves as part of Islam's campaign of conquest — its *Dar-al-Harb*.

Islam sees its mission as unfolding in three stages: the *Dar-al-Suhl* in territories which Islam has yet to conquer; the *Dar-al-Harb* in territories in the process of being conquered; and the *Dar-al-Islam*, in which Islam has succeeded in subjugating the non-believers. Every year there is published in Egypt an Islamic yearbook. This year's edition designates France, Belgium, and the United Kingdom as territories at the *Dar-al-Harb* stage. This, then, is the situation in which we are at present. One should not forget that during the riots [of November 2005] two Catholic churches were destroyed. Dalil Boubakeur (the imam of Paris' Great Mosque) condemned these church burnings, but he didn't excommunicate those responsible for them. It was also the first time that public buildings were attacked and burned: police stations, public schools, etc. This has been made light of [in the public sphere], but it's heavy with significance. It is also the first time that people were killed — four to be exact . . .

Menzo: What do you see as the cause for this?

Guillaume Faye: One cause is mass, unbridled immigration. In Canada, for instance, immigrants are selected according to their profession, their wealth, and their economic potential. We, on the other hand, have let in massive numbers of immigrants from rural [Third World] economies whose customs and cultures are totally different from our own, who are entirely unprepared for what they will encounter here, and who lack any of the proper educational or professional requisites [for integration]. Who could possibly think that this would work? — even with the gigantic investments the state has made in housing, education, and special programs for them. Japan is about as wealthy as we are, but it has hardly any immigrants; and those few it has cannot count on the slightest state support. In France, by contrast, the number of young people of foreign origin will virtually double in the next ten years. Integration is not working. The politicians refuse to acknowledge the catastrophic implications of their policies. Most are concerned only with their careers. Some are too old to even care. Why should Chirac [the French president] worry about what will happen in ten years? — he'll probably be dead by then. Besides, politicians look at the population as an electorate [made up of voters who can be periodically replaced]. Distinct peoples, however, are not interchangeable. They belong to well-defined cultures and are attached to the mentalities in which they were formed. A Brazilian is simply not interchangeable with a Russian. Only the politicians seem not to realize this.

Another cause for the riots is the increased number of sub-Saharan Africans. These groups will cause even greater problems in the future

Menzo: Why?

Guillaume Faye: Because, unlike Maghrebian immigrants [Arabs from Algeria, Morocco, and Tunisia], they are completely desocialized. The Maghrebian population possesses a definite family structure, with a father and a mother. In sub-Saharan countries, such structures are non-existent. Mothers can have children with different fathers and children are raised [not by the family, but] by the village. When such familial structures are exported to a city like Paris, it inevitably produces problems. Paris is not a village and the rearing of children is not its responsibility. The [offspring of these Africans] frequently turn to crime and end up in the justice system. They don't know who their father is and no one takes responsibility for them. Their presence here is like a time bomb.

Menzo: You've pointed out that from 1989 to 1999, the rate of juvenile crime [in France] increased 176 percent and that the number of those convicted have tripled. You don't attribute this growth to unemployment. What is its cause?

Guillaume Faye: There are two reasons why crime is increasing. The first is social heterogeneity. Every diverse population has problems with criminality. The two countries with the lowest levels of crime are those with the most homogeneous population: Japan and Costa Rica. Aristotle was the first to note that a society cannot be democratic and harmonious if its population is not homogeneous. Without such homogeneity, it becomes tyrannical. The second cause of criminality stems from the permissiveness of those responsible for maintaining order: the police and the courts. In Tunisia, there's massive unemployment, but crime is relatively minor because the police and the courts react to it with severity. In Saudi Arabia, you can leave your keys or your wallet in the car and no one would think of stealing them — otherwise they might have their hands cut off. With us, on the contrary, foreigners experience a situation where, since 1968, all forms of punishment have, in effect, been rejected.

Menzo: You have also written that crime will finance the impending race wars. Do you really think there is a plan for this?

Guillaume Faye: It's not only been planned, it's already happening. Police reports show that criminal gangs are now helping finance the insurgency in Iraq. Of course, not all criminals are participating in this, but it exists. And they [the authorities] think it is possible to buy social peace! It is estimated that three tons of cannabis are distributed every month in the Paris suburbs. Another source of funding is stolen cars and a third is the trafficking of electronic goods. Prostitution is also a source of revenue, as well as arms dealing. Whenever the authorities discover a [criminal] arsenal, it includes not only military arms, but also hunting rifles, which are ideal for urban warfare.

Menzo: In your book [*Avant-Guerre*], you put Islam on the same level as other ideologies that seek to rule the world: Communism, American liberalism/globalism, etc. But isn't history a long succession of systems and ideologies that seek world domination?

Guillaume Faye: Not at all. Look at Judaism, which is an ethnic religion and has no intention of converting the rest of the world to its belief system. Neither Buddhism nor Shintoism seeks world conquest. But Islam does, as did Catholicism, Communism, and neo-liberalism. Islam, though, is the most aggressive of all these. For it is not simply a religion, but a political doctrine. And this doctrine is imperialist. Twice before in history it has sought to conquer Europe. The first time it was stopped by Charles Martel at Poitiers [in 732]; the second time, in the Seventeenth century, it was beaten back at the gates of Vienna. Islam's present conquering ambition was revived in Egypt in the 1920s. I'm convinced that certain Islamic leaders believe the moment is now right for a third offensive against the West. As the former Algerian president Houari Boumediène once boasted, the Islamic world today carries in the wombs of its women the weapons that will conquer Europe.

Menzo: The first generation of immigrants displayed absolutely no hostility to us. The third generation seems more segregated than ever. Is this the result of the Palestinian conflict, which has generalized anti-Western behaviors? Is this the source of the current problem and is there a solution to it?

Guillaume Faye: It's certainly one of the sources, but it's hardly the only one. Even before the Palestinian conflict, anti-Western hatred was ripe. It stemmed in part from the hatred colonization had fostered. But opposition to the West also arose from jealousy [of Western achievement] . . . The Palestinian conflict has certainly acted as catalyst for hatred, but even if it were resolved tomorrow, there would still be a problem. Europe is also despised because it is weak and emasculated. Its permissiveness invites indulgence, which makes us an easy target. Muslims find themselves in a society that is morally degenerate. One philosopher recently evoked the Hindu notion of the Kali Yuga — the Age of Iron. According to this ancient prophecy, there will come a time when men will marry men and women women, the kings will become thieves and the thieves kings, and mothers will kill their babies in their wombs. *Eh bien*, we are not too far from this.

Menzo: In your book, you put the Belgium situation on a par with the French one. Belgium, however, lacks France's massive, alienating housing projects. Our immigrants usually reside in Nineteenth-century urban quarters, which have maintained [their human character] and are largely free of the 'no-go zones' that [make the French situation so dangerous]. In your view, how is Belgium threatened?

Guillaume Faye: You're right. The French *banlieues* [with their modernist housing estates] are unique. They were constructed to house French refugees from Algeria. In the course of a single week [in 1962], a million Frenchmen were evacuated from [newly-independent] Algeria. It should be emphasized, though, that these projects built to accommodate this influx were not at all disagreeable, for there was then a good deal of money available to finance their construction. At the same time, new residential towns (such as Paris Deux, near

Versailles) were built to house not foreigners but the well-heeled middle-class. This is quite different from the situation in Brussels, today the symbolic capital of Europe and the seat of NATO. But what counts [is not the housing situation *per se*] but the fact that a massive part of population is non-European . . .

Menzo: Do you think, then, that riots will eventually break out in Brussels?

Guillaume Faye: As I see it, it is only a matter of time . . . Though Brussels is perhaps better situated than Paris, it is not likely to be spared.

Menzo: In the United States and Britain, there are periodic outbreaks of rioting, but these are usually between rival ethnic gangs. In France, the riots were directed against the state itself. Police and firemen were shot at and attacked. How did it come to this?

Guillaume Faye: In the United States, there is, for example, increased conflict between Blacks and Mexicans. In France, on the other hand, non-French gangs turn [not on one another, but] on France itself. Rap music has had a role to play in this. Rap's subversive effect should not be dismissed. But more, these immigrant gangs find themselves in France because France has helped them; [the resentment this causes] is something distinct to the Maghrebian/Islamic mentality. It's a very peculiar sentiment, but is nevertheless something that has to be accounted for. You hate those who help you, because you feel humiliated when helped. The more they are coddled, the more, then, they are likely to react aggressively. Besides, empathy isn't fostered by weakness. In promising immigrants more aid and money after the riots, the Villepin government acted unwisely . . .

Menzo: Besides more riots and urban warfare, you predict an escalation in the nature of terrorist attacks: micro-, macro-, and giga-terrorism, including the possible use of nuclear weapons against the United States. Do you really think this is possible?

Guillaume Faye: Naturally. The scenario I've depicted is not far from being realized. In time, all these things will be possible. We can expect something a hundred times worse than 9/11. It's only a matter of time.

Menzo: You've criticized the intelligence services for a lack of imagination and vigor. You've said that they are not reflective enough and have not fully understood the different modes of fundamentalist belief. However, nearly every month the intelligence services manage to foil various planned terrorist assaults. Is the peril really as great as you claim?

Guillaume Faye: You need to distinguish between the maintenance of order and the collection of intelligence. Western intelligence agencies have done much good work in both areas. They have managed to break up numerous clandestine cells and terrorist groups. But more is needed. It is necessary to have a large, well-informed group devoted to this. You also need to have the means and personnel in place to quickly sound the alarm. This is how the terrorist assault on the Strasbourg Cathedral was foiled. You also need to capitalize on terrorist mistakes. Prior to 9/11, a female employee in a private pilot school reported that certain students were devoting all their time to learning how to fly and not to take off and land. Only months after the fact did anyone pick up on this . . . Believe me: the unthinkable is going to become thinkable. What Baghdad experiences every day, we will soon know.

National Vanguard, January 8, 2006

French version: 'La troisième guerre mondiale va commencer' (January 7, 2006) (http://be.altermedia.info)

8

GUILLAUME FAYE AND THE JEWS

Few postwar thinkers in my view have played a greater role in ideologically resisting the forces assaulting Europe's incomparable bioculture than Guillaume Faye. This was publicly evident at the international conference on 'The White World's Future' held in Moscow in
June of this year, which he helped organized. It's even more evident
in the six books he's written in the last seven years and in his innumerable articles, interviews, and conferences in which he has alerted
Europeans to the great challenges threatening their survival.

In this spirit he has developed an 'archeofuturist' philosophy that
takes its inspiration from the most primordial and Faustian urgings
of our people's spirit; he has incessantly warned of the threat posed
by the Third World, especially Islamic, invasion of the former white
homelands; he has promoted European collaboration with Russia and
made the case for an imperium stretching from Dublin to Vladivostok;
he privileges biopolitics over cultural or party politics; he's developed
a theory of the interregnum that explains why the existing system of
subversion will soon collapse; and he's successfully promoted anti-
liberal ideas and values in a language and style that transcends the
often ghettoized discourse of more sectarian tendencies.

Despite his incomparable contribution to the forces of white
resistance, he has always remained suspiciously silent on certain key
issues, particularly regarding the Jews, the so-called Holocaust, and
the interwar heritage of revolutionary nationalism — even though he
is routinely referred to in the mainstream media as a 'fascist', a 'racist', and a 'Holocaust denier'. On those few occasions he has spoken of
Israel or the Jews, it has been to say that their cause is not ours and that

we need to focus on the dangers bearing down on us. To this degree, his silence seemed perfectly reasonable. Recently, however, he's broken this silence to take a stance likely to alienate many of his supporters. The occasion was an interview granted to the Zionist 'France-Echos'. When asked about anti-Semitism in the 'identitarian' movement he influences, Faye responded in explicitly philo-Semitic terms: 'Anti-Judaism (a term preferable to anti-Semitism) has melted away like snow in the sun. There are, of course, pockets of resistance . . . But this tendency is more and more isolated . . . because of the massive problem posed by Islamization and Third World immigration. In such circumstances, anti-Judaism has been forgotten, for the Jew no longer appears as a menace. In the milieu I frequent, I never read or hear anti-Jewish invectives. . . . [A]nti-Judaism [he claims] is a political position that is now obsolete, unhelpful, out of date, even when camouflaged as anti-Zionism. This is no longer the era of the Dreyfus Affair. Anti-Jews, moreover, are caught in an inescapable contradiction: they despise Jews, but claim they dominate the world, as if they were a superior race. This makes anti-Judaism a form of political schizophrenia, a sort of inverted philo-Semitism, an expression of *ressentiment*. One can't, after all, detest what one aspires to . . . My position is that of Nietzsche: To run down the Jews serves no purpose, it's politically stupid and unproductive'.

Besides ignoring the fact that Jewish lobbies have never been more dominant and destructive, three questions, I see, are raised in this quote:

1. Is it that the problems posed by immigration and Islam have trivialized those once associated with the Jews?

2. Or is it that Islam and immigration reveal that the Jews are not (and never were) a problem, that the anti-Judaism of the Dreyfus era, like other historical expressions of anti-Judaism, was simply a product of a culture whose traditionalism or resentment 'stupidly' demonized the Jew as the Other?

3. Or is it that one can't have two enemies at the same time, that the threat posed by Islamic immigration is greater than whatever threat organized Jewry might pose, making it strategically necessary to focus on the principal enemy and to relegate the other to a lesser degree of significance?

Faye tends to conflate these questions, leaving unsaid what needs to be said explicitly. He assumes, moreover, that the Islamic or Third World threat (both in the form of the present invasion and internationally) is somehow unrelated to Jewish influence. He acknowledges, of course, that certain Jews have been instrumental in promoting multiracialism and immigration. But the supposition here is that this is just a tendency on the part of certain Jews and that to think otherwise is to commit the error of seeing them in the way that 'old fashion' anti-Semites once did. At first glance, his argument seems to be that of Jared Taylor and American Renaissance, being a tactical decision to take the path of least resistance. Faye, though, goes beyond Taylor, making claims about the Jews that will inevitably compromise his standing among many of his readers.

The anti-Islamism and philo-Semitism that Faye here combines reflect a deeper ideological divide in French nationalist ranks. This divide is symptomatic of a schism that is rarely discussed by anti-system nationalists, but has had worldwide ramification for our movement. Since 1945, when the anti-white forces of triumphant American liberalism and Russian Communism achieved world hegemony, the hounded, tattered ranks of the nationalist right, in Europe and America, split into a number of divergent, if not contradictory tendencies. With the advent of the Cold War and the formation of the Israeli state, these tendencies tended to polarize around two camps. One tendency, including certain former National Socialists, allied with postwar anti-Communism, viewing the Russian threat as the greater danger to Western Civilization. Given Israel's strategic place in the Cold War alignment, these anti-Communists treated Zionism as an ally and downplayed the 'anti-Semitism' that had traditionally been part of their anti-liberal nationalism. This tendency was opposed by another, which also included former National Socialists, but it saw Russian Communism in terms of Stalin's alleged anti-Semitism and nationalism. This led it to assume an anti-American, anti-Zionist, and pro-Third World position.

The legacy of this polarization continues to affect ethnonationalist and identitarian ranks, even though their elements have been jumbled and rearranged in recent years. As ideal types, however, neither tendency is completely supportable. Euro-nationalism, as well as white nationalism, I suspect, will succeed as movements only in synthesizing the pro-white elements of each tendency and discarding their pro-Third World ones. For a long time, I thought Faye represented an ideal synthesis of this heritage, for he was pro-Russian without being hysterically anti-American; anti-Third World without supporting the globalist superstructure dominating the 'West'; anti-modern and postmodern in the Maistrian sense. More impressive still, his orientation was to a revolutionary, ethnonationalist, and archeofuturist concept of Europe that refused any accommodation with the reigning powers.

Recently, however, his anti-Islamism seems to have morphed into a Zionism that cannot but trouble ethnonationalists and identitarians. In the 'France-Echos' interview, he says in reference to his nationalist critics that it is nonsensical to call him a Zionist since he is not a Jew. But in the same breath he adds: 'How could I be anti-Zionist? . . . Unlike Islamism, Communism, Leftism, human rights, and masochistic, post-conciliar Christianity, Zionism neither opposes nor restrains in any significant way the ideals I defend, that is, the preservation of [Europe's biocultural] identity. How would the disappearance of Israel serve my cause? For a European identitarian to think the Hebrew state is an enemy is geopolitically stupid'. He goes on to argue that those who are viscerally anti-American and anti-Zionist are implicitly pro-Islamic, pro-Arab, and immigrationist, allies in effect of the Left's Third Worldism. Pointing to Alain de Benoist's GRECE, Christian Bouchet's revolutionary nationalists, and those 'Traditionalist' European converts to Islam, all of whom are fascinated by Iran's new leadership and by Hezbollah, he claims, with some justice, that these anti-Zionists are in the process of abandoning their commitment to Europe.

Faye's contention that Islam (the civilization) is a mortal threat to Europe is well grounded. While one might appreciate Ahmadinejad's critique of Zionist propaganda, especially as it takes the form of the Holohoax, or Nasrallah's humbling of the IDF, to go from there to supporting Iran's Islamic Republic or Islamic insurgents in general (think of the Paris Ramadan uprising of November 2005) is, for ethnonationalists and identitarians, a betrayal of another sort. Faye here acts as an important bulwark against those in identitarian ranks who would leave it to others to fight their battles — others, if history is any guide, who won't hesitate to subjugate them once the opportunity arises.

Where Faye crosses the line in my view is in arguing that Jews ought to be considered a native part of European civilization, that the defense and reinforcement of the Zionist state is vital to Europe, and that Israel is the vanguard in the struggle against 'our common enemy'. Israel's collapse, he argues, would 'open the door to the total conquest of Europe'. He concludes by declaring that he is no Judeophile. 'I consider the Jews allies, as part of European civilization, with a very particular and original status as a people apart'. He rejects anti-Judaism 'not because it is immoral, but because it is useless, divisive, infantile, politically inconsistent, outdated'. For ostensively strategic reasons, then, he rejects what he calls 'anti-Judaism'.

* * *

It is not my intention here to critique Faye's new-found Zionism (which, I think, is insupportable for a 'nationalist') — that would require a format different from this report. It is also not my intention to put his other ideas in doubt, for I continue to believe that he has made an incomparable intellectual contribution to the cause of European resistance. I do, however, question how Faye can consider a non-European people like the Jews to be part of Europe's biocivilization; how he can ignore the destructive role they or their powerful lobbies have often played in European and especially American history; how he can dismiss their role in fostering the anti-white forces of multiculturalism, globalism, and the existing regime; and how he can think that Israel is not a geopolitical liability to Europe and Russia?

Finally, I can't help but recall an earlier occasion when Faye argued that our survival as a people depended on 'ourselves alone' — and not on appeals to those whose interests are inevitably served at our expense.

Vanguard News Network, July 31, 2006

9

THE NEW JEWISH QUESTION
OF GUILLAUME FAYE

Apropos of Guillaume Faye, *La Nouvelle question
juive*. Chevaigné: Éds. du Lore, 2007.

*'I don't know whether God loves or hates the English;
I only know that they must be driven out of France.'*
— Saint Joan

In his critique of this controversial book, the Swiss 'revisionist'
scholar Jürgen Graf, now exiled in Russia, writes that Guillaume
Faye has permanently discredited himself 'in racial nationalist and
nationalist circles worthy of the name'.[1] The reason: his 'dishonest'
and defamatory attack on those who challenge the Holocaust Story
and on those who uphold the traditional 'Judeophobic' orientation of
the nationalist right.

The New Jewish Question (henceforth NJQ) may indeed mark
the end of Faye's career as a leading identitarian and nationalist
ideologue among certain segments of the racially conscious community — though by no means all of it. For the sharp differences pit-
ting the holocaust-debunking exile against the militant anti-Islamic

---

1   Jürgen Graf 'The New Jewish Question, or The End of Guillaume Faye', http://www.
    adelaideinstitute.org/LEGAL2006/Faye.htm; my quotations come from the French
    original, 'La Nouvelle question juive ou la fin de Guillaume Faye', http://www.
    juergen-graf.sled.name/articles/graf-la-fin-de-guillaume-faye.html. Cf. 'Dr. Robert
    Faurisson on Guillaume Faye', http://www.thecivic platform.com/2007/11/23/
    dr-robert-faurisson-on-guillaume-faye-2/; Michael O'Meara, 'Guillaume Faye and
    the Jews', http://www.vanguardnewsnetwork.com/?p=841.

Frenchman reflect differences that divide nationalists throughout Europe, as long-standing historical-ideological identities closely associated with the anti-liberal wing of the nationalist Right clash with the electoral imperatives of national-populist parties endeavoring to stem the pro-immigrant policies of their respective states.[2] The white man's future may hinge on how these differences are resolved.

The Argument

Faye's anti-revisionism is part of a larger argument related to what he claims is the changing Jewish relationship to white society.

Central to this change is the Third World colonization of the European heartland — and all the world-destroying effects that have followed in its wake.

Since the late 1990s, as the colonizers became bolder and more assertive, attacks on French Jews (in the form of vandalized synagogues, school violence, murder, etc.) have steadily risen. The mainstream media routinely denounces the 'radical Right', but these attacks are largely the work of Muslim immigrants. Still of 'low intensity', Faye claims they are symptomatic of a new, more virulent anti-Semitism, which mixes anti-Zionist politics with the Koran's traditional ethnocidal aversion to the Jews, threatening in this way to move Europe closer to Eurabia.

In appraising this new phenomenon, Faye, who has long been persecuted by Jewish advocacy groups for his anti-system 'nationalism', professes to be neither pro- nor anti-Jewish. His single avowed concern as a writer and activist is the survival of Europe. In his treatment of the NJQ, he thus fully acknowledges that the Jews are not 'white' (i.e., not of European Christian descent) and that their relationship with European society has often been negatively affected by their 'schizophrenic' attitude toward Europeans (or what Kevin MacDonald more forthrightly calls their ethnocentric 'double

---

2   For disclosure's sake, I should mention the divided loyalties affecting my review of this work. Revisionism, especially as disseminated by Mark Weber's Institute for Historical Review, played a major role in shaping my work as a professionally-trained historian and as a ethnonationalist; relatedly, revisionist ideas led to the termination of my short-lived academic career. My identification with Graf is thus both personal and intellectual. At the same time, I helped introduce English-speaking nationalists to Faye's ideas, which I continue to think are an invaluable contribution to the coming European Revolution.

standard').[3] He also acknowledges that the Jewish Question was once 'pivotal to the issue of European, especially French, identity, for, historically, the Jews were seen as the *métèque* (i.e., the 'wog', the 'wop', the offensive foreigner) who threatened the corruption of the nation's blood and morals' (p. 23).

Given the present Third World inundation, the Jews, he argues, can no longer seriously be taken as either an alien menace or a *métèque*, especially considering that more and more of them are allegedly beginning to doubt the wisdom of open borders. Not a few nationalists and identitarians have consequently abandoned their traditional anti-Semitism. The Vlaams Belang, Europe's most successful nationalist formation, has, for example, formed a tacit alliance with the Jewish community of Flanders in order to stem the nation's Islamization; he also cites the Jews' role in Jared Taylor's American Renaissance and could have mentioned Griffin's BNP, Fini's National Alliance, Kjaersgaard's Danish People's Party, and many others.

Anti-Jewish hatred nevertheless persists on the nationalist Right, in Faye's view distorting its movement and distracting it from its principal tasks.

He also claims that nationalist and far Right anti-Semites have, in face of the invasion, altered their view somewhat, seeing Jews less as an immediate physical threat than a pernicious influence — as Zionism or elite social engineering — responsible for policies, immigration pre-eminently, that threaten white survival. Contemporary anti-Jewish ideology, as a result, now rests on three general tenets: that 1) the Jews dominate the world through the cultural and financial powers they wield; that 2) they are the principal force promoting white decadence; and that 3) they immunize themselves to criticism through their manipulation of the Holocaust Story. Much of the NJQ seeks to refute these tenets, revealing not just their alleged political inappropriateness to the nationalist cause, but their role in occulting the challenges facing it. More specifically, the NJQ seeks to sever all association with historical anti-Semitism, the Third Reich, and everything else that might prevent Europeans from joining nationalists in repelling the Muslim advance. In the name of political realism, then,

---

3   Kevin MacDonald, *The Culture of Critique: An Evolutionary Analysis of Jewish Involvement in Twentieth-Century Intellectual and Political Movements* (Bloomington: 1stBooks, 2002).

Faye makes a case for abandoning principles and positions that Graf, among others, considers essential to the nationalist project.

Decadence

The poorly researched and poorly argued case Faye makes in support of his argument, especially regarding the third tenet, is amply demonstrated in Graf's review and need not be rehashed here. Two larger and equally serious questions raised by Faye do, however, deserve revisiting, namely: 1) are the Jews, traditional purveyors of anti-ethnic, anti-racial, and cosmopolitan principles, the cause of the white man's present decline, and 2) are the Jews, as the most influential group in society, the principal enemy in the battle for white survival?

In respect to the first question, Faye says that the decadence of white societies may have been promoted by certain Jewish intellectuals, but its real origins lie in the inner recesses of the European soul — specifically in the secular and religious distillations of Christianity. Jews, in other words, have only exacerbated tendencies already indigenous to white life.

The French Catholic Church, he points out, dwarfs French Jewish efforts in promoting not just open borders, race mixing, and pro-immigrant policies, but cosmopolitanism, universalism, and a self-denying love of the Other.

Faye's argument here is certainly correct in claiming that the *ultimate* responsibility for white race replacement lies with whites and that Christianity, along with its various secular offshoots (egalitarianism, individualism, universalism, etc.), have had a terrible effect on white identity, helping foster processes destructive of both Europe's organic and cultural substratum.

The problem with this aspect of Faye's argument is that Catholicism, like other forms of Christianity, is a temporal institution subject to history. As such, it has been different things in different periods. Thus it was that Bishop Turpin in *La Chanson de Roland* confronted the 'Saracens' as a 'Christian' warrior bearing the arms of the Frankish hero cult, while Episcopalians in the antebellum South defended the legitimacy of Negro slavery with chapter and verse. Even if the argument is only that the deep structure of Christian belief harbors an anti-white or anti-ethnic impetus, it still doesn't explain why

for centuries it served an opposite purpose. Finally, and most impor-
tantly, it was the secularization of Christian belief, associated with
modernization, that provoked (or, at least, marked the beginning of)
the 'crisis of Western man' and the subsequent assault on the unique
worth of his specific being — and not Christianity itself.[4]

In a similar way, it needs adding, this historical factor also affects
the anti-Semitic argument. When Jew-hatred shed its religious forms
in the latter part of the Nineteenth century, becoming an 'anti-Semitism' (implying a critique of Jewish behavior) instead of an anti-Judaism (implying a critique of Jewish religion), it did not explain why
the Jews' anti-gentile disposition (which, after all, had been around
since the Hellenistic Age) was suddenly hegemonic. Many of the great
anti-Semites (e.g., Proudhon, Dühring, Drumont, Sombart, etc.) consequently directed their critique not just against the Jews but against
those European elites who collaborated with them and especially
against the emerging social-economic order which fostered such collaboration and made the Jews alleged subversion possible. (Hence, the
prominence of anti-Semites in Nineteenth- and Twentieth-century
anti-modernist movements.) The point here is that this 'people
that shall dwell alone' may have evolved a psychology destructively
opposed to white society — a psychology, given its biological foundation, that transcends historical contingencies — but in itself this
doesn't explain why in one period Jews were fleeing pogroms and in
another managing the White House.

Faye is much more convincing when he emphasizes those larger
processes that turned Europeans against themselves, noting that the
history leading to the white man's present self-destruction — the history whose distant origins reside in the Renaissance, the Reformation,
and the French Revolution and whose most imposing forms were
philosophically expressed in the Enlightenment, politically in liberalism, and economically in capitalism — was part of a long, complex
chain of causes and effects that cannot seriously be attributed to a
Jewish conspiracy. Egalitarianism, human rights, materialism, individualism, and the categorical imperative, moreover, may all have
been promoted by Jewish intellectuals at the white man's expense,

---

4   This is not an apology, but a simple historical observation — one, moreover, made
    with the knowledge that most non-Orthodox distillation of Christianity are today
    objectively anti-white and that, at the same time, any credible nationalist movement
    in America or Europe cannot be anti-Christian.

but to think that they are not pre-eminently products of European culture is possible only through an ignorance of that heritage. The sources of what Faye calls the present decay lie, as a consequence, as much in ourselves as elsewhere.[5] Since Jews, then, are only the occasional instrument of this historical subversion, they are no worse than the multitude of whites who also serve the subversive forces. To blame them for the predicament we're in is not only false, Faye insists, but dishonorable.

There is a truth in this, just as vulgar or obsessive anti-Semitism which attributes all the white man's woes to the 'highly ethnocentric, Christian-hating' Jews is something of a bugaboo, justifying its critics' contempt. But there is nevertheless reason for seeing the forces assaulting white life and culture as Judaic in spirit — in the sense that they either stem directly from the Jews' innate hostility to white Christians, reflect the white man's embrace of Jewish behavioral norms, or constitute part of the Jews' millennia-long campaign against Europe's traditions, aristocracies, symbols, and transcendent values.[6] Relatedly, it seems hardly coincidental that for millennia European peoples designated the *esprit juif* — the spirit of 'rule breakers, border crossers, and go-betweens' — as not just alien to their own, but as destructive to their unique 'synthesis of spirituality and virility'. (The more extreme forms of this designation have gone so far as to link Jews with 'those cosmic forces which are destructive and evil and inimical to human life'.) This still doesn't make the Jews the chief source of white decadence and Faye is certainly correct in

---

5   In probing the sources of European decay, our greatest thinkers are closer to Faye than to the anti-Semitic vulgate: think of Nietzsche's theory of nihilism, Weber's Iron Cage, Heidegger's concealing of being, Spengler's organic cycles, or Evola's loss of Tradition — all of which emphasize the self-destructive tendencies inherent in European culture. Kevin MacDonald's own work, in considering the role that individualism, weak ethnocentrism, and moral universalism have played in making whites vulnerable to Jewish subversion, also acknowledges the effects of these European sources (though he emphasizes the primacy of the Jewish ones).

6   When Slezkine argues (further substantiating MacDonald's argument in *The Culture of Critique*) that the 'Modern Age is the Jewish Age', he affirms, in effect, the essentially Judaic character of the existing system. Yuri Slezkine, *The Jewish Century* (Berkeley: University of California Press, 2004). Julius Evola, arguably the most profound anti-Jewish critic of the Twentieth century, actually ended up abandoning his anti-Semitism after 1945 because he thought it 'absurd' to continue posing the Jewish Question when the 'negative behavior attributed to Jews had become that of the majority of Aryans'. Julius Evola, *Il Cammino del Cinabro* (Milan: Scheiwiller, 1972). Also Michael O'Meara, 'Evola's Anti-Semitism', (Forthcoming: November 3, 2007), *The Occidental Quarterly Online* (http://toqonline.com).

emphasizing that Europeans have never needed them to engage in ethnomasochistic behavior — for the entire course of modern, especially Twentieth-century, history has been cause enough. But it does suggest, though Faye doesn't quite agree, that white and Jewish spirits have been historically opposed and that the hegemony of the latter cannot but have a distorting effect on white being. Indeed, it is the white man's alienation from his inmost spirit that arguably causes him, as Heidegger says, to 'fall out of being' and thus into decay, decline, and decadence.[7]

Revealingly, Faye ignores the fact that anti-Semitism appears in virtually every period of European history. He understands the Jewish Question only as a facet of Nineteenth- and early Twentieth-century developments and does so without actually examining the nature of our increasingly Hebraicized world. Moreover, it is only the Jews' 'schizophrenia', the divided loyalties they harbor toward Europe, that he sees as arousing European hostility and provoking gentile opposition. Though acknowledging the often negative offshoots of this 'schizophrenia', he also claims it is nowhere near as threatening as the menace posed by Islam and that it is frequently mitigated by the Jews' identification with 'Western Civilization'. Faye thus joins those nationalists who seek 'freedom from history' in order to pursue anti-immigrationist politics without being associated with the demobilizing tags of anti-Semitism, National Socialism, racism, and extremism, dismissing, in effect, the contention that it's the anathematization of these earlier expressions of European being that empowers and legitimates the system's anti-European policies.

It would be historically unserious, I believe, to dispute Faye's claim that the Jews are not wholly responsible for the white man's decline. But at the same time it is quite another thing to then claim, as Faye does, that the Jewish Question is today *passé* and of no political interest to the struggle for white survival. There's a difference, he ignores, between discarding the baggage of the past and avoiding the challenges the past poses to the present. A case in point is the Holocaust Story, whose misrepresentation, as Graf, among others, points out, is used to defame Europe's greatest people, the Germans, demonizing not

---

7   Martin Heidegger, *Introduction to Metaphysics*, trans. Gregory Fried and Richard Polt (New Haven: Yale University Press, 2000).

only their history and *ethnos*, but that of all Europeans. A European nationalist movement to stave off the race's destruction by accepting this defamation and demonization, along with the lies, propaganda, and repression accompanying them, might arguably enhance its electoral prospects, but the proponents of such a system-accommo-dating movement never seem to concern themselves with the kind of 'nationalism' it would represent or the sort of goals it could possibly achieve — or if it would actually be able to address the real sources of European decay. Again, following Heidegger, I would go further and argue that Europe and the 'West' will never be reborn without the spiritual rebirth of the Germans ('the people of the center') and that this is impossible as long as they are forced to cower in shadow of the Holocaust Story.

The Enemy

Of even greater concern for Faye is his belief that nationalists and identitarians fixated on the Jewish Question ignore the real enemy: the non-white Muslim hordes encamped on Europe's southern border who threaten to replace the indigenous European population.

Confronted with 6 million non-whites inside France and the millions to arrive in the near future, Faye argues that 600,000 French Jews (the largest Jewish community in Europe) are hardly an enemy. He even argues that the power and influence of France's Jewish minority, virtually omnipotent in anti-Semitic eyes, are wan-ing. Unlike the Nineteenth and first half of the Twentieth century, Jews no longer dominate the nation's financial heights, having been supplanted by the holders of Anglo-American pension funds, Arab petrodollars, and the new East Asian economies; he also stresses that none of the world's top 50 banks are Jewish owned. Likewise, in French education, the judiciary, the unions, and the civil ser-vice, Jewish power is marginal and in French politics, ideas, and media, while still prominent, is hardly dominant. Possessing pow-ers incommensurate with their demographic weight, these powers are not, then, what they once were. Future trends (world opinion's increasingly negative image of Israel, European Islamization, the rise of the East Asian powers and their non-Eurocentric world order, etc.), Faye insists, will exacerbate this tendency. At the same time,

Jews are allegedly becoming less and less supportive of mass Third World immigration.[8] In a period when Europe is under assault by Islam, revisionism and other anti-Jewish engagements, he argues, are 'a typical example of a phony problem, a strategy of avoidance, of taking shelter in the past' (p. 171).[9] Anti-Semitism, in a word, has become 'an ideological relic of a dead past', irrelevant to the great challenges posed by the rising tide of color.

I suspect readers of this review will find this a strange argument, given that Jewish power in the U.S. has never been greater or more destructive and that even France, the one European country not completely subject to American hegemony, has recently been captured by 'semi-neocons'.[10] How, then, can Faye, given his history and publishing record, make such a claim? One obvious reason, touched on above, is that anti-Jewish politics have the effect of politically marginalizing nationalists and that for them to break out of their ghetto they need to conform to the system's underlying principles or else risk continued irrelevance. His argument (which is not entirely wrong) nevertheless rests on the assumption that the European situation is roughly analogous to the American one. Jewish power in Europe, however, has never been as great as its American counterpart and has a different nature, for this power is a product of the American-centric system introduced in 1945—a system, I would argue, whose deracinating, globalizing, and totalizing economic and technological tendencies are pre-eminently Jewish and cosmopolitan, though it takes an ostensively American form (Graf describes

---

8   Evident in the immigration policies of Nicolas Sarkozy, French Jews are becoming less supportive of the present Afro-Arab immigration, which is the principal source of the growing anti-Semitism. But this does not mean, as Faye assumes, that they are beginning to oppose Third World immigration *tout court*. Rather, Sarkozy's 'select immigration' increasing orients to East Asians, who are both less of a welfare charge and indifferent to Judaism. Michael O'Meara, 'Racial Nationalism and the French Presidential Election of 2007', http://www.vanguardnewsnetwork.com/?p=1703.

9   This argument bears comparison to the argument he makes against European anti-Americanism. See Guillaume Faye, *Le Coup d'État mondial: Essai sur le Nouvel Impérialisme Américain* (Paris: L'Æncre, 2004); Michael O'Meara, 'Europe's Enemy: Islam or America?', *The Occidental Quarterly* 5, no. 3 (Fall 2005).

10   'Semi' because *Sarko l'Américain* has on several occasions threatened to mutate into *Sarko l'Européen*—given that the geopolitical imperatives of France's leadership of Europe overrides the pro-Americanism of his neocon ideology. See 'Candide postmoderne, avec Ray-Bans, jean's et "esprit apocalyptique"' (January 11, 2008), http://www.dedefensa.org/article,php?art_id=4819.

it as 'a Frankenstein monster with a non-Jewish body and a Jewish head').[11]

Given the power of the system's centripetal forces and the degree to which the old European order was destroyed during the Second World War (and thus the degree to which it is no longer possible to speak of Europe as an autonomous actor), Faye in my view underestimates the external (American) sources of Jewish influence. For this system — which today subjects the entire planet to its 'democratic' terrorism — is geared to the transnational imperatives of U.S. planners, which has the effect of subordinating Europe to its inherently Judeo-American logic. When Faye points out that France's pro-immigration policies were mainly the work of gentiles and that countries like Ireland or Spain, with negligible or non-existent Jewish communities, have enacted similar ethnocidal policies, he is quite right to argue that Jewish involvement, if any, was peripheral. Nevertheless, the anti-European system prompting the implementation of these policies — the system which transferred sovereignty from the nation-state to the New World's global economic order — is very much Jewish (and American) in depriving whites of everything that might prevent their submersion in its great coffee-colored market.[12] In effect, Europe's philo-Semitic policies are facets of the 'invisible empire' to which its comprador elites are irreparably tied and this empire (with its liberal-capitalist impetus and often Jewish leadership) is inherently disposed to destroying the white man's 'racial and blood values'. Faye, in fact, has himself in numerous previous works emphasized the degree to which the United States has lobbied, if not compelled, Europeans to promote multiculturalism, mass Third World immigration, and Muslim Turkey's admission to the EU.[13]

---

11 The history of this system has yet to be written. It was anticipated as early as 1950 in Carl Schmitt, The Nomos of the Earth in the International Law of the Jus Publicum Europaeum, trans. G. L. Ulmen (New York: Telos Press, 2006 [1950]). Its origins have been examined in Jean-Gilles Malliarakis, Yalta et la naissance des blocs (Paris: Éds. du Trident, 1995 [1982]). One of its better recent theoretical conceptualizations is Alexandre Zinoviev, La grande rupture: Sociologie d'un monde bouleversé, trans. Slobodan Despot (Lausanne: L'Âge d'Homme, 1999). Faye himself attempted to grasp the system's nature in one of his more important early works, Le Système à tuer les peuples (Paris: Copernic, 1981).

12 Julius Evola, Three Aspects of the Jewish Problem (n.p.: Thompkins & Cariou, 2003).

13 'What we call Americanism is nothing else . . . than the Jewish spirit distilled'. Werner Sombart, The Jews and Modern Capitalism, trans. M. Epstein (New Brunswick: Transaction Books, 1982 [1911]), 38. Writing at the beginning of the

All this is mentioned by way of getting to Faye's most important question: Who is the enemy?

From the Schmittian perspective of Twentieth-century nationalism, the designation of the enemy is at the heart of every *grande politique*. 'The enemy', Carl Schmitt writes, 'exists only when . . . one fighting collectivity of people confronts a similar collectivity'.[14] Historically, the enemy was a rival state that threatened one's survival. But the political — which poses man's highest existential tasks — is invoked whenever friend/enemy polarities come into play, and threaten 'to negate an opponent's way of life'.[15] That the question of race replacement touches on the continued existence of the white biosphere makes racial politics 'political' in the highest sense.

Even though 'some' Jews continue to employ their double standard, Faye believes they are not the life and death threat that the non-white invaders pose. And though their open border advocacy and their pathologization of white identity have helped foster conditions facilitating the replacement of the indigenous white population, Faye questions if this makes the Jews a greater threat than the Third World interlopers — who are presently ethnically cleansing neighborhoods, disrupting traditional ways of life, and de-Europeanizing Europe. Worse, an obsession with Jews has caused not a few nationalists to ally with their enemy — the Muslims, who are qualitatively more anti-white and supremacist than the Jews. (The latest, most disastrous example of this was the 2007 presidential campaign of Le Pen's National Front.) He claims, moreover, that the Jews (specifically their intellectuals) are not solely responsible for opening the gates to the 'barbarians', that they have in fact been joined by other, often more consequential, white culprits, and that to waste energy focused on their gate-opening activities is to neglect the real danger lurking in the suburbs and on the border. If nationalists are to mount an effective resistance to the anti-European forces, it is imperative, Faye insists, that they jettison their anti-Semitism and wage their struggle within the system's philo-Semitic terms.

Twenty-first century, MacDonald makes a similar contention in *The Culture of Critique*. The difference is that Sombart, the century before, believed the liberal-capitalist core of American civilization was inherently Judaic, while MacDonald contends that it was imposed.

14 Carl Schmitt, *The Concept of the Political*, trans. George Schwab (Chicago: University of Chicago Press, 1996), 28.

15 Schmitt, *The Concept of the Political*, 27.

There is both a political and a theoretical issue at stake here. In our postmodern age, when the *jus publicum Europaeum* has given way to globalism's anti-European *nomos*, nationalists confront a situation where they are obliged to fight a multi-front, asymmetrical war: against an external enemy, the non-white hordes replacing Europeans, and against an internal enemy, those liberal elites, Jewish or otherwise, who promote and make possible this replacement. Faye and the reformists focus on the external enemy, his critics, like Graf, on the internal enemy. The question inevitably arises, though: Who is the principal enemy, the gatekeepers or the gatecrashers?

For Faye, it's the non-white immigrants and every distraction from this realization is a step closer to the European's impending Islamization. For Graf, it is the system responsible for the Third World invasion. 'Effective struggle against immigration within the current framework', he writes, 'is totally impossible. In order to stop the invasion the system has to be overthrown either by a popular insurrection or a *coup d'état*'. This is a revolutionary answer that strikes at the root of the problem.[16] Such an anti-institutional answer is one, though, that neither Faye nor the 'conservative' majority in national-populist ranks is presently willing to entertain — if for no other reason than it slights the visible enemy and complicates white efforts to reform existing policies.

How one sees the system affects, then, how one defines the principal enemy. And how one sees the Jews in relation to the system decides if this makes them the principal enemy or not. To the degree, therefore, that the *esprit juif* is the system's spirit and favors specifically Jewish interest at the expense of white ones, the Jews are the real danger. But — and this is the qualification that muddies the water — to the degree that it is the system itself, independent of the Jews, that is responsible for our predicament and thus the degree to which the Jews are only one of its instruments, then they are just facets of a larger, more complex web of subversion — which makes them an adversary to be sure, and one with a very distinct visage, but not, in themselves, the principal enemy.[17]

---

16 Cf. Michael O'Meara, 'The Northwest Novels of H. A. Covington', http://www. counter-currents.com/2010/11/the-northwest-novels-of-h-a-covington/; and Michael O'Meara, 'Against White Reformists', http://www.counter-currents.com/2012/07/ against-white-reformists/.

17 For decades now, the Jewish spirit has obviously influenced the 'hostile elite' managing America's world system, but whether this power elite is Jewish in essence is something that anti-Jewish critics have yet to prove.

There is, admittedly, nothing neat and tidy in this, yet it is characteristic of late Twentieth-century politics that nationalists are compelled to fight both foreign invaders and their own collaborating ruling class.[18] The totalizing character of such struggle, with its universalization of enmity and its confusion of opponents, again owes a great deal to the final breakdown of the Eurocentric system of nation-states after 1945, for, in addition to threatening the existence of white people and denying a future to their children, this breakdown completely undermined the traditional European 'bracketing' of war — to such an extent that it now increasingly pits the state against the nation, conflates the forces of civil war, revolution, and national liberation, and entails a struggle that is as much about class as it is about race.[19] This makes it very difficult to designate the principal enemy. It also raises a question of the highest political order, which Faye neglects entirely: for instead of exonerating the Jews, whose collaboration with the system is either necessary or sufficient to its purpose, and instead of abandoning the lessons of the European past, which offers numerous historical examples of successful anti-system struggles, Faye might have asked if anything meaningful can possibly be accomplished within a system that he himself once described as 'the destroyer of nations' (*le tueur des peuples*).

The Occidental Quarterly 7, no. 3 (Fall 2007)

---

18 Think of France in the early Sixties, when General Salan's Organisation Armée Secrète had to fight a non-white enemy in Algiers and a French enemy in Paris; or the situation today in Iraq, as Sunni insurgents simultaneously battle Shi'ites, the puppet government in Baghdad, and the foreign army of occupation.

19 Carl Schmitt, 'Theory of the Partisan', *Telos*, no. 127 (Spring 2004).

10

FOREWORD TO THE ENGLISH
TRANSLATION OF *ARCHEOFUTURISM*

'We have kept faith with the past,
and handed down a tradition to the future.'
— Patrick Pearse, 1916

Guillaume Faye was long associated with that school of thought, which the French media in 1978 labeled *'la nouvelle droite'* — though it was Right-wing in no conventional sense, representing, as it did, the distinctly postmodern cause of 'European identitarianism'.

Not to be confused with the various neoliberal, implicitly Protestant, and market-oriented tendencies bearing the same designation in the English-speaking world, the French New Right grew out of the GRECE (the Groupement de Recherche et d'Études pour la Civilisation Européenne), an association formed in 1968 by various anti-liberals hoping to overcome the failed legacies of Pétainism, neo-fascism, Catholic traditionalism, regionalism, colonialism, and Poujadism — in order to resist the cancerous Americanization of their homeland.

To this end, the GRECE's founders believed they would never over-throw America's liberalizing hegemony, as long as the general culture remained steeped in liberal beliefs. In the formulation of its master thinker, Alain de Benoist: 'Without Marx, no Lenin'. That is, without the ascendance of anti-liberal ideas in the general culture and thus without a revolution of the spirit, there would be no viable movement against *le parti américain*.

The GRECE was established, thus, not for the sake of *la politique politicienne*, but for metapolitically rearming European culture.

And in this, it was not unsuccessful. For the GRECE's philosophically persuasive revival of anti-liberal thought and the subsequent affiliation of several prominent European thinkers to its banner made it an influence of some immediate import. Indeed, it can almost be said that for the first time since the Action Française, 'Rightists' in the '70s, led by Alain de Benoist, achieved a level of sophistication and attraction nearly 'comparable' to that of the Left, as France's 'intellectual Right' threw off the defenseless conservatism that came with Americanization to challenge the liberal consensus imposed after 1945.

* * *

While still working on his doctorate in Political Science at the prestigious Institut d'études politiques de Paris (Science Po), Guillaume Faye began gravitating to the GRECE. By 1973, he had become its 'number two' advocate, a role he would play until 1986.

Like other *Grécistes* in this early period, Faye was influenced by those European currents that had previously countered the imposition of liberal ideology.

Foremost of these counter-currents were the Conservative Revolution of the German 1920s (Spengler, Moeller van den Bruck, Schmitt, Freyer, Heidegger, Jünger, etc.); the Traditionalism of Julius Evola; the Indo-Europeanism of Georges Dumézil; the heritage of pre-Christian paganism; and tellurocratic geopolitics.

Contemporary anti-liberal ideas in stream with these deeper currents — such as the ethology of Konrad Lorenz or the philosophical anthropology of Arnold Gehlen — were similarly incorporated into the GRECE's anti-liberal curriculum.

Faye, though, took to these ideas differently (more radically, in my view) than the GRECE's leader, Benoist — perhaps because of his earlier affiliation with the Situationists and the 'aristocratic' ex-Communist Henri Lefebvre; more probably because of his apprenticeship with the Italian journalist, Germanist, and post-fascist firebrand Giorgio Locchi; and ultimately, of course, because of his specific temperament.

Less prolific and encyclopedic than Benoist, the younger Faye was considered by some the more creative (*le véritable moteur intellectuel de la nouvelle droite*). He was obliged, though, to play second fiddle to the master, who seemed bent on blunting the edge of New Right radicalism. There was, as a consequence, a certain implicit tension between their contrary notions of the anti-liberal project.

* * *

For reasons explained in the first chapter of *Archeofuturism*, Faye quit the GRECE in 1986. During the next dozen years, he worked in 'media' as a radio personality, journalist, entertainer and, alas, an occasional pornographer. The publication of *L'Archéofuturisme* in 1998 signaled his return to the metapolitical fray.

At one level, this work accounts for the dead-end Benoist's GRECE had gotten itself into by the mid-1980s, suggesting what it could have done differently and with greater effect.

At another, more important level, it addresses the approaching *interregnum*, endeavoring to 'transcend' the historical impasse that pits the ever changing present against the immense heritage of the past.

To this end, archeofuturism calls for 'the re-emergence of archaic configurations' — pre-modern, inegalitarian, and non-humanist — in a futuristic or long-term 'context' that turns modernity's forward, innovative thrust (totally nihilistic today) into a reborn assertion of European being, as the temporal and the untimely meet and merge in a higher dialectic.

Archeofuturism is thus both archaic and futuristic, validating the primordiality of Homer's epic values in the same breath it advances the most daring contemporary science.

Because the Anglophone world outside the British Isles is a product of liberal modernity, the struggle between tradition and modernity, pivotal to Continental European culture, has been seemingly tangential to it.

This struggle nevertheless now impinges on the great crises descending on the U.S. and the former white dominions.

Faye's archeofuturism holds out an understanding of this world collapsing about us, imbuing European peoples with a strategy to think through the coming storms and get to the other side — to that post-catastrophic age, where a new cycle of being awaits them, as they return to the spirit that lies not in the past *per se*, but in advance of what is to come.

Saint Ignatius of Loyola Day, 2010

11

PROPHET OF THE FOURTH AGE: INTRODUCTION TO *WHY WE FIGHT*

'L'histoire est la réalisation des idées irréalisables.'
— Guillaume Faye

Are these the last days of Europe?
There's no hyperbole here.[1] If major changes are not soon forthcoming, her peoples face the extinction of their civilization and their kind. Already she is overrun by millions of alien, mainly Islamic colonizers from the Global South, who have begun to replace her native peoples and supplant her order; she is subject to an American overlord whose world system (of which the EU is its foremost part) requires her de-Europeanization and 'globalization'; she is misgoverned by technocrats, career politicians, and plutocratic elites indifferent to her blood and spirit. And to all this (to which much could be added), her defenders — those who sense the danger and strive to resist it — are disunited, at times even unaware of who or what exactly they are fighting. Within a generation, 'Europe' may go the way of Ancient Sumer or the Incas.

Guillaume Faye — the one-time *enfant terrible* of France's Nouvelle Droite — believes the 'European Resistance' has the resources and energies to defeat the Continent's enemies, *if* its various elements and tendencies should form a united front around clear ideas and a common ideology. That is, if her defenders would agree to concentrate their forces. His manifesto, and especially its ideological dictionary,

---

1   Walter Laqueur, *The Last Days of Europe: Epitaph for an Old Continent* (New York: St. Martin's Griffin, 2009).

aspire to lay the metapolitical foundations for such a unification — by designating and defining the key ideas and ideology that will make it possible.

* * *

Why We Fight (as *Pourquoi nous combattons*) appeared a decade ago, in 2001. In a few places it shows its age, but much of it seems prescient in its understanding of the challenges confronting Europe's defenders and the ideas that might overcome them. These 'defenders', whom Faye collectively labels the 'resistance', include in their ranks *néo-droitiers*, regionalist, identitarian, traditionalist, and certain other anti-system tendencies upholding the primacy of their particular ethnic distillation of the larger European heritage. A decade after *Why We Fight*, these oppositional elements (the 'resistance') have finally begun to emerge from their political ghetto, as they hesitantly mobilize in the streets and, more confidently, merge with the national-populist formations affecting the present fate of parliamentary coalitions.[2] It's fitting, perhaps, that the English translation of Faye's manifesto should appear in this period of rising anti-system agitation.

Influenced by the cultural/ideological forces animating the mounting opposition, *Why We Fight* followed a series of works that had earlier lit up the resistance's imagination. These were the essays collected in *L'Archéofuturisme* (1998); the second, augmented edition of *Nouveau discours à la nation européenne* (1999); and *La Colonisation de l'Europe* (2000) (whose critical characterization of Europe's Islamization earned Faye and his publisher a 300,000 franc fine and a year's suspended sentence).

Why We Fight would be followed by a series of similarly topical and prophetic works: *Avant-Guerre* (2003), *La Convergence des catastrophes* (2004), and *Le Coup d'État mondial* (2004). But then, in 2007, the release of Faye's most controversial book, *La Nouvelle question juive* (in which the Jew's place in European life was reconceived in light of the Islamic invasion), set off a heated debate in identitarian

---

2 Fondation Robert Schuman, 'L'Union européenne face aux défis de l'extrémisme identitaire' (July 12, 2010), http://www.robert-schuman.eu/question_europe. php?num=qu-177. Also Stéphane François, 'Réflexions sur le mouvement "identitaire"' (March 3, 2009), http://tempspresents.wordpress.com/2009/03/03/reflexions-sur-le-mouvement-identitaire-12/.

and nationalist ranks — eventually bringing his role as the resistance's leading advocate to an end.[3]

If Faye's decision in the period leading up to 2007 — to affiliate with the Zionist bloc in its 'struggle' against Islam — discredited him with certain identitarians,[4] it took away nothing from his earlier contribution to the 'resistance' — which seems especially the case with *Why We Fight*, arguably the single best synthesis of the ideas and sensibilities animating the diverse parties and tendencies resisting Europe's decline.

* * *

The reception of Faye's 2007 book on the Jews epitomized much of what has stunted the postwar history of European anti-liberalism.

Following V-E Day, the Right, like the rest of Europe, was ordered to Americanize. Joseph Stalin (whose Red Army won the all-important ground war) may have foiled U.S. efforts after 1945 to create a 'new world order' (forcing globalists to wait until 1989),[5] but the American conquerors managed to impose their liberal-modernist system on Western and Central Europe (this anti-European market system which has since evolved into the basis of the present global market order).

Traditional Right-wing formations critical of the creedal, market-centric dictates of Europe's new masters would henceforth be identified with the 'allegedly' barbaric Germans,[6] escorted offstage, and

---

3 On the links between the Zionist far Right and the European, especially French, nationalist far Right, see Pierre Vial, 'Grandes manoeuvres juives de séduction à l'égard de l'extrême droite européenne', *Terre et Peuple*, no. 44 (Summer 2010).

4 Michael O'Meara, 'Guillaume Faye and the Jews' (July 31, 2006), http://www.toqonline.com/blog/guillaume-faye-and-the-jews/; Michael O'Meara, 'The New Jewish Question of Guillaume Faye', *The Occidental Quarterly* 7, no. 3 (Fall 2007).

5 K. R. Bolton, 'Origins of the Cold War: How Stalin Foiled a "New World Order"' (May 31, 2010), http://www.foreignpolicyjournal.com/2010/05/31/origins-of-the-cold-war-how-stalin-foiled-a-new-world-order/.

6 'Allegedly' in the sense that the Americans, Russians, and British, unlike the Germans, waged the war as altar boys — i.e., in a sense that goes beyond all reference to National Socialism. For in the spirit of liberalism's self-righteous, despiritualized Protestant suppositions, it inevitably treats every form of anti-liberal ideology as an inhuman malignity, whose only remedy is extermination. See Carl L. Becker, *The Heavenly City of the Eighteenth-Century Philosophers* (New Haven: Yale University Press, 1932); Joseph de Maistre, 'Sur le Protestantisme' (1798), in *Oeuvres*, ed. Pierre Glaubes (Paris: Laffont, 2007); Carl Schmitt, *The Concept of the Political*, trans. George Schwab (Chicago: University of Chicago Press, 1996 [1927]), 53-58.

compelled to abandon whatever anti-liberal or anti-modern sentiment still influenced them — as was the case in Eastern Europe, though there the model was Russian, rather than American.

By the time the first postwar baby boomers came of age in the late Sixties, it was evident that the Right (this now 'moderate' appendage of the liberal Left) was a losing proposition, having failed not only to halt the ongoing erosion of European civilization, but having, more shamefully, joined the American system de-Europeanizing Europe — betraying, in this way, the purpose of 'the political' — by failing to defend Europe's identity, legitimacy, and sovereignty.

Across the Continent in the Sixties and Seventies, but especially in France, there emerged tendencies endeavoring to rethink the Right project as an alternative to the prevailing U.S. system (which makes the circulation of capital superior to everything, including the sacred). The most successful of these alternatives was the Groupement de Recherche et d'Études pour la Civilisation Européenne (GRECE). Its project, of which Faye was an early advocate, was 'metapolitical': i.e., conceived as a cultural/ideological struggle against the reigning liberal values and beliefs. By means of this 'Gramscianism of the Right', Grécistes were to create a 'counter-hegemony' to undermine the legitimacy of the subversive forces — and thus to create a climate receptive to an anti-liberal politics of reconquest.

Effective at first in arousing public debate and reviving aspects of the repressed cultural heritage, the GRECE by the mid-1980s had evolved into just another marginalized tendency. In his recently translated *Archeofuturism*,[7] Faye attributes this to its proclivity, especially pronounced in its leader, Alain de Benoist, to privilege the 'meta' in metapolitics at the expense of 'the political', which has had the effect of making cultural/ideological engagement a substitute for, rather than an active facet of politics.[8]

---

7 Guillaume Faye, *Archeofuturism: European Visions of the Post-Catastrophic Age*, trans. Sergio Knipe (London: Arktos, 2010), 23-51. Also Robert Steuckers, 'Les pistes manquées de la "nouvelle droite": Pour une critique constructive' (2009), http://euro-synergies.hautetfort.com/archive/2009/08/28/les-pistes-manquees-de-la-nouvelle-droite-pour-une-critique.html.

8 Alain de Benoist, 'Les causes culturelles du changement politique' (1981), in *La Ligne de mire, 1972-1987* (Paris: Le Labyrinthe, 1995); Georges Gondinet, 'Les ambiguïtés du "gramscianisme du droite"', *Totalité: Révolution et Tradition*, no. 10 (November 1979).

At one level, Faye's *Why We Fight* is a blistering critique of Benoist's leadership of the GRECE. Its many negative references to 'the Right' or to 'certain Right-wing intellectuals', etc., are aimed, almost exclusively, at him and the type of politically irrelevant, often system-friendly dilettantism he has come to represent for Faye.

The book's numerous references to Pierre Vial and Robert Steuckers, on the other hand, point to what Faye considers a more viable metapolitics. An academic historian and former president of the GRECE, Vial left the group in the late 1980s to join the National Front, where he organized its Terre et Peuple (Land and People) faction,[9] which helped shift the NF away from its earlier Jacobin-Reaganite nationalism and toward the socially-conscious, identitarian populism that has since made it the leading party of the French working class.[10] Steuckers, a Flemish linguist and arguably the most formidable intellectual talent to emerge from the Nouvelle Droite, is the organizer of *Euro-Synergies*—which synthesizes and diffuses much of the most significant thought influencing European anti-liberalism.[11]

* * *

'*Today, as always, the corner-stone of society is a tombstone*'.[12]

In assuming the inextricability of culture and politics, Faye's notion of metapolitics stems from his 'archeofuturist' philosophy, which holds that the European tradition is pre-eminently a 'revolutionary' one—constantly revolving back to its archaic sources in order to revolve forward, toward another, original expression of it. In Italian terms, his archeofuturism combines the revolutionary traditionalism of Julius Evola and the radical futurism of F. T. Marinetti. Less simply put, it marries the perennial attributes of, say,

---

9   Pierre Vial, *Une terre, un people* (Paris: Éds. Terre et Peuple, 2000). The Terre et Peuple website is at http://terreetpeuple.com/.

10 Sylvain Crépon, 'Le tournant anti-capitaliste du Front National' (2006), http://tempspresents.wordpress.com/2010/04/25/sylvain-crepon-tournant-anti-capitaliste-du-front-national/.

11 Steuckers' two websites are *Euro-Synergies*, at http://euro-synergies.hautetfort.com/, and *Vouloir*, at http://vouloir.hautetfort.com/.

12 Guglielmo Ferrero, *Words to the Deaf: A Historian Contemplates His Age*, trans. Ben Ray Redman (New York: Putnam, 1926), 116.

the Greco-Roman classical heritage[13] to the most pioneering forms of European thinking and endeavor.[14] Like the primordial and the perennial, the archaic here refers not to some ancient, fossilized canon, but to the original assertion of European being, which, as an origin (an outburst or a birth of being), functions as another original opening to the future — in the structuring, civilizing sense distinct to Europe's *Hochkultur*. It's not, as such, a traditionalism, an antiquarianism, or a reactionism — but rather a primordialism that constantly renews Europe's rooted life forms by adapting them to the challenges coming from the future.

In opposing modernity's dysgenic values for the sake of those instincts and refinements that have historically guided the Continent's destiny, Faye's archeofuturism strives — in its conception of the world — to revive the European's threatened identity, to pull him back from the abyss into which he presently gazes, but, above all, to make certain he gets another chance, a fourth chance, to begin again.

* * *

The present counter-civilization, whose reality-denying entertainments, obsessive consumerism, and nihilistic miscegenation have drained all meaning from our world — this liberal-modernist system that came with the ruin of Europe's Ancient and Medieval civilizations — is not the 'enemy', however, for (in any political, especially Schmittian, sense) the enemy has to be someone or something ('a fighting collectivity of people') threatening imminent death.[15]

Faye also refuses a certain tendency to blame America for the Continent's vassalage and her capitulation to the North African Arabs and sub-Saharan Blacks (the '*Beur-Blacks*') colonizing her native lands and exploiting her permissive society.[16]

---

13 Faye did ten years of Greco-Latin studies with the Jesuits responsible for educating the children of the high Parisian bourgeoisie.

14 A literary example of this can be found in Joyce's *modernist* masterwork, *Ulysses*, which retells the founding story of European man, utilizing 'mythopoeic imagery, structured features, formal principles, plotting elements, and linguistic resources' taken from the earliest Greek and Irish myths. See Maria Tymoczko, *The Irish Ulysses* (Berkeley: University of California Press, 1994), 1.

15 Schmitt, *The Concept of the Political*, 28.

16 Michael O'Meara, 'Europe's Enemy: Islam or America?', *The Occidental Quarterly* 5, no. 3 (Fall 2005).

Europe for him has no one, ultimately, but herself to blame for the policies and social practices now destroying who she is (i.e., her identity).

At the same time, and with greater conviction, Faye believes a very real flesh-and-blood enemy — *un corps étranger et parasitaire* — mortally imperils Europe: the replacement populations gathered under the Prophet's banner.

America may collude with the forces of Islam to divide and weaken Europe for the sake of her global empire,[17] and liberal modernist illusions may lead European elites to believe the Islamic colonizers can be integrated without destroying her historic family of nations — but neither of these things, in Faye's view, quite makes them an 'enemy'.

Europe's liberal-modernist elites and America's world empire, Faye argues, are 'adversaries' of Europe — they exploit and manipulate her, but pose no direct threat to her physical existence. Islam and the peoples of the Global South, by contrast, constitute precisely such a threat, for these alien forces have explicitly designated her as the enemy they intend to destroy.[18] In colonizing European lands and replacing her native peoples, they have, in fact, already begun turning Europe into a *Dar-al-Islam*[19] — which is eventually going to turn the Continent into an anti-Europe.

The question of Islam also affects many of the sectarian divides running through the 'resistance'. Some, like *Grécistes*, look on tradition-minded Islam as a possible ally in the struggle against the destructuring forces of America's anti-European world order.[20] Allied with Muslim anti-modernists opposing Americanization, global capitalism, and the prevailing liberal-managerial system, these

---

17 Alexandre Del Valle, *Islam et États-Unis: Une alliance contre Europe* (Lausanne: L'Âge d'Homme, 1997).

18 Bat Ye'or, *Eurabia: The Euro-Arab Axis* (Madison: Fairleigh Dickinson University Press, 2005); also Guillaume Faye, *La Colonisation de l'Europe: Discours vrai sur l'immigration et l'Islam* (Paris: L'Æncre, 2000).

19 Serge Trifkovic, *The Sword of the Prophet* (Salisbury: Regina Orthodox Press, 2007).

20 Alain de Benoist, *Europe, Tiers monde, même combat* (Paris: Robert Laffont, 1986); more recently, 'Interview mit Alain de Benoist', *Hier & Jetzt*, no. 15 (July 14, 2010). Cf. Martin Lichtmesz, 'Alain de Benoist unter Muslimen und Mauertaniern' (July 27, 2010), http://www.sezession.de/17988/alain-de-benoist-unter-musilimen-und-mauretanien.html.

néo-droitistes[21] assume a stance almost antipodal to Faye's[22] — with much of the 'resistance' occupying places somewhere between their respective polarities.

Faye's argument seems most convincing in emphasizing that the Barbarians crashing the City's gates pose an immediate danger of the highest priority. His view of this danger is, perhaps, more insistent than that of any other commentator. His argument, though, is a good deal less persuasive when minimizing the danger that comes from within the City — i.e., the danger that comes from the European elites who have opened the City's gates to the Barbarians. It's as if the 'enemy' for him — the one who creates a state of emergency threatening everything — can only be an external (non-European) rather than an internal (European) one (though he's fully acknowledges the self-destructive character of late modernity). For this reason, he sees these elites as an accessory (i.e., something secondary) to the real danger — the gatekeepers being thus less of a threat than the gatecrashers. But here again his critics have trouble distinguishing between the danger posed by the gatekeepers, who make the invasion possible by opening the City gates, and the more obvious danger posed by the menacing gatecrashers already within the City's walls.

However consequential and often unpleasant these differing anti-system orientations have been in fostering sectarian rifts within the 'resistance', they detract little from the quality of Faye's *Manifesto* or from the 177 key terms he develops to conceptualize and articulate its metapolitical project.

* * *

To appreciate something of its foresight, the reader might recall the historical context in which *Why We Fight* appeared.

---

21 Bereft of a historical project and nostalgic for the good old days of the Popular Front, the Left (it still calls itself this!) continues to see Adolf Hitler lurking in the GRECE's shadow, but the establishment (which has realized much of the Left's historic project) is increasingly less critical of it. Jean-Yves Camus, 'La Nouvelle droite: Bilan provisoire d'une école de pensée', *La Pensée*, no. 345 (January-March 2006), now certifies it as 'system friendly'.

22 On Benoist's ethnopluralist rejection of identitarianism, see Michael O'Meara, 'The Faye-Benoist Debate on Multiculturalism' (May 11, 2004), http://foster.20megsfree.com/468.htm; Michael O'Meara, 'Benoist's Pluriversum: An Ethnonationalist Critique', *The Occidental Quarterly* 5, no. 3 (Fall 2005); Michael O'Meara, 'Community of Destiny or Community of Tribes?', *Ab Aeterno*, no. 2 (March 2010).

For the identitarian, anti-system Right, it was a period ideologically rearmed with the rediscovered heritage of the Conservative Revolution, the great, philosophically unassailable anti-liberal achievement of the German 1920s, but it was also no less important as a period whose postmodernist stirrings seemed to pose the possibility of another Conservative Revolution.[23]

For the system, never more triumphalist, it was the everything-is-going-right period before the Islamic terrorist attack of '9/11' and the ensuing production known as the Global War on Terrorism — the period before the hubristic violence of George Bush's 'shock and awe' overextended the American empire, preparing its present breakdown — before September 2008, when the supposedly irreversible progression of the global market came to a sudden, economy-wrecking standstill (as 'the dream of global free market capitalism died')[24] — and before October 2010, when the German Chancellor, Angela Merkel, model of the postwar, American-centric sense of propriety, declared that multiculturalism had 'totally failed' and that immigrants had better start assimilating.

Besides anticipating the devastations accompanying globalism's 'end of history', Faye's *Why We Fight* caught a glimpse of the larger metahistorical logic that was then, and is still, leading the American-centric world system to disorder and possible collapse — the logic he calls the 'convergence of catastrophes' (the same system-destroying logic that some label the 'Collapse', the 'Long Descent', the 'Long Emergency', the 'End of Oil', the 'Coming Anarchy', etc.).

When the *Manifesto* appeared in 2001, unregulated global market practices were considered as 'inevitable' as the 'end of history' that came with Communism's fall; similarly, 'hi-tech' and the digitization of financial capitalism were heralded as the economic equivalent of the Second Coming. But most emblematic of the period, Bill Clinton ('America's first Black President') assumed the leadership of what was to be a post-European, post-ideological, and post-historical stage in human development, in which the United States — drunk on

23 Javier Esparza, 'Le pari de la post-modernité' (1986); Claudio Risé, 'La postmodernité est une révolution conservatrice!' (1997); Robert Steuckers, 'La genèse de la postmodernité' (1989), at http://vouloir.hautetfort.com/archive/2011/02/10/pm.html

24 Martin Wolf, 'The Rescue of Bear Stearns Marks Liberalisation's Limit', *Financial Times*, March 26, 2008.

its unipolar ideal of power and believing its virtual ideals (the 'end of history' pre-eminently) were somehow immune to reality — sanctimoniously assumed heaven's mandate to safeguard its 'new order of the ages'. In the name of the world's sole superpower, successor of Rome, this mandate would lead it to wage 'humanitarian wars' (Serbia, Kosovo, Iraq, etc.) in the name of its disordering *nomos*; to enthrone abstract, disembodied 'human rights' everywhere at the expense of historic and customary rights; to prevent all regulation of High Finance or Wall Street, and to use its vast powers to uphold the claim that the U.S. economy (and, by implication, the U.S. itself) had evolved, as the former Chair of the Federal Reserve (Alan Greenspan) put it in 1998, 'beyond history'[25] (i.e., beyond the realities that normally condition economic/political behavior); etc.

Against the Babbitts of the so-called Right (whose one and only God is Mammon) and against the Philistines of the Marxist Left (who betrayed the European working class for the detritus of an overpopulated Third World), Faye saw that the anti-European, multicultural, reality-denying forces of America's global economic order would experience (within a decade) not just a long patch of very stormy weather, when its fantasy projects and hyper-power plans would succumb to certain formerly-denied realities — he saw that its self-generating catastrophes, and the interregnum they would create, were about to give the 'resistance' another opportunity to throw off liberalism's death-embrace — and, once the chaos passed, inaugurate a Fourth Age of European Civilization.[26]

San Francisco, January 2011

---

25 'Statement by Alan Greenspan before the Joint Economic Committee, U.S. Congress, June 10, 1998', http://www.federal.reserve.gov/boarddocs/testimony/1988/199806.10htm.

26 Charles Lindholm and José Pedro Zúquete, *The Struggle for the World: Liberation Movements for the 21st Century* (Stanford: Stanford University Press, 2010); Michael O'Meara, 'Against the Armies of the Night: The Aurora Movements' (June 21, 2010), http://www.counter-currents.com/2010/07/against-the-armies-of-the-night/.

12

SEX AND DERAILMENT

Apropos of Guillaume Faye, *Sexe et dévoiement.*
Chevaigné: Éds. du Lore, 2011.

Four years after Guillaume Faye's *La Nouvelle question juive* (2007) alienated many of his admirers and apparently caused him to retreat from identitarian and Euro-nationalist arenas, his latest work signals a definite return, reminding us of why he remains one of the most creative thinkers opposing the system threatening the European race.

In this 400-page book, which is an essay and not a work of scholarship, Faye's main concern is the family, and the catastrophic impact the rising number of divorces and broken households is having on white demographic renewal. In linking family decline to its demographic (and civilizational) consequences, he situates his subject in terms of the larger social pathologies associated with the 'inverted' sexuality now disfiguring European life. These pathologies include the devirilization and feminization of white men, the normalization of homosexuality, feminist androgyny, Third World colonization, spreading miscegenation, the loss of bio-anthropological norms (like the blond Jesus) — and all that comes with the denial of biological realities.

At the core of Faye's argument is the contention that sexuality constitutes a people's fundament — by conditioning its reproduction and ensuring its longevity. It is key, as such, to any analysis of contemporary society.

As the ethologist Konrad Lorenz and the philosophical anthropologist Arnold Gehlen (both of whom have influenced Faye) have demonstrated, there is nothing automatic or spontaneous in human sexuality, unlike other animals. Man's body may be like those of the higher mammals, but it is also a cultural, plastic one with few governing instincts. Socioeconomic, ideological, and emotional imperatives accordingly play a major role in shaping human behavior, especially in the higher civilizations.

Given, moreover, that humanity is an abstraction, there is no universal form of sexual behavior, and thus the sexuality of Europeans, like everything else, differs from that of non-Europeans. In the United States and Brazil, for example, the Negro's sexual practices and family forms are still very unlike those of whites, despite ten generations in these European-founded countries. Every form of sexuality, Faye argues, stems from a specific bioculture (a historically-defined 'stock'), which varies according to time and place. Human behavior is thus for him always the result of a native, inborn ethno-psychology, historically embodied (or, like now, distorted) in the cultural, religious, and ideological superstructures representing it.

The higher, more creative the culture the more sexuality tends to depend on fragile, individual factors (desire, libido, self-interest), in contrast to less developed cultures, whose reproduction relies more on collective and instinctive factors. High cultures consequently reproduce less and low cultures more — though the latter suffers far greater infant mortality (an equilibrium upset only in the Twentieth century, when intervening high cultures reduced the infant mortality of the lower cultures, thereby setting off today's explosive Third World birthrate).

Yet despite these significant differences and despite the world's great variety of family forms and sexual customs, the overwhelming majority of peoples and races nevertheless prohibit incest, pedophilia, racially mixed marriages, homosexual unions, and 'unparented' children.

By contravening many of these traditional prohibitions in recent decades, Western civilization has embarked on a process of 'derailment', evident in the profound social and mental pathologies that follow the inversion of 'natural' (i.e., historic or ancient) norms — inversions, not incidentally, that have been legitimized in the name of morality, freedom, equality, etc.

Sexe et dévoiement is an essay, then, about the practices and ideologies currently affecting European sexuality and about how these practices and ideologies are leading Europeans into a self-defeating struggle against nature — against *their* nature, upon which their bio-civilization rests.

The Death of the Family

Since the Cultural Revolution of the 1960s, numerous forces, expressive of a nihilistic individualism and egalitarianism, have helped undermine the family, bringing it to the critical stage it's reached today. Of these, the most destructive for Faye has been the ideology of libidinal love (championed by the so-called 'sexual liberation' movement of the period), which confused recreational sexuality with freedom, disconnected sex from reproduction, and treated traditional social/cultural norms as forms of oppression.

The Sixties' 'liberationists', the first generation raised on TV, were linked to the New Left, which saw all restraint as oppressive and all individuals as equivalent. Sexual pleasure in their optic was good and natural, and traditional sexual restraint bad and unnatural. Convinced that all things were possible, they sought to free desire from the 'oppressive' mores of what Faye calls the 'bourgeois family'.

'Sexual liberation', he notes, was 'Anglo-Saxon' (i.e., American) in origin, motivated by a puritanism (in the Nineteenth-century Victorian sense of a prudery hostile to eroticism) that had shifted from one extreme to another. Originally, this middle-class, Protestant prudery favored a sexuality whose appetites were formally confined to the 'bourgeois' (i.e., the monogamous nuclear) family, which represented a compromise — between individual desire and familial interests — made for the sake of preserving the 'line' and rearing children to carry it on.

In the 1960s, when the Boomers came of age, the puritans passed to the other extreme, jettisoning their sexual 'squeamishness' and joining the movement to liberate the libido — which, in practice, meant abolishing conjugal fidelity, heterosexual dominance, 'patriarchy', and whatever taboos opposed the 'rationally' inspired, feel-good 'philosophy' of the liberationists. As the Sorbonne's walls in '68 proclaimed: 'It's prohibited to prohibit'. The 'rights' of individual desire and happiness would henceforth come at the expense of all the prohibitions that had formerly made the family viable. (Faye doesn't mention it, but at the same time American-style consumerism was beginning to take hold in Western Europe, promoting a self-indulgent materialism that favored the egoistic pursuit of pleasure. It can even be argued, though again Faye does not, that the state, in league with the media and the corporate/financial powers, encouraged the permissive consumption of goods, as well as sex, for the sake of promoting the market's expansion.) If Americans pioneered the ideology of sexual liberation, along with Gay Pride and the porn industry, and continue (at least through their Washingtonian Leviathan) to use these ideologies and practices to subvert non-liberal societies (which is why the Russians have rebuffed 'international opinion' to suppress Gay Pride parades), a significant number of 'ordinary' white Americans nevertheless lack their elites' anti-traditional sexual ideology — as Salt Lake City prevails over Las Vegas.

Europeans, by contrast, have been qualitatively more influenced by the 'libertine revolutionaries', and Faye's work speaks more to them than to Americans (though it seems likely that what Europeans are experiencing will sooner or later be experienced in the United States).

Against the backdrop, then, of Sixties-style sexual liberation, which sought to uproot the deepest traditions and authorities for the sake of certain permissive behaviors, personal sexual relations were reconceived as a strictly individualistic and libidinal 'love' — based on the belief that this highly inflated emotional state was too important to limit to conjugal monogamy. Marriages based on such impulsive sexual attractions and the passionate 'hormonal tempests' they set off have since, though, become the tomb not just of stable families, but increasingly of Europe herself.

For with this permissive cult of sexualized love that elevates the desires of the solitary individual above his communal and familial attachments (thereby lowering all standards), there comes another kind of short-sighted, feel-good liberal ideology that wars on social, national, and collective imperatives: the cult of human rights, whose flood of discourses and laws promoting brotherhood, anti-racism, and the love of the Other are synonymous with devirilization, ethnomasochism, and the destruction of Europe's historic identity.

Premised on the primacy of romantic love (impulsive on principle), sexual liberation has since destroyed any possibility of sustaining stable families. (Think of Tristan and Iseult.) For its sexualization of love (this 'casino of pleasure') may be passionate, but it is also transient, ephemeral, and compelled by a good deal of egoism. Indeed, almost all sentiments grouped under the rubric of love, Faye contends, are egoistic and self-interested. Love in this sense is an investment from which one expects a return — one loves to be loved. A family of this kind is thus one inclined to allow superficial or immediate considerations to prevail over established, time-tested ones. Similarly, the rupture of such conjugal unions seems almost unavoidable, for once the pact of love is broken — and a strictly libidinal love always fades — the union dissolves.

The subsequent death of the 'oppressive' bourgeois family at the hands of the Sixties' emancipation movements has since given rise to such civilizational achievements as unstable stepfamilies, no-fault divorce, teenage mothers, single-parent homes, abandoned children, a dissembling and atavistic 'cult of the child' (which esteems the child as a 'noble savage' rather than as a being in need of formation), parity with unisex ideology, a variety of new sexual categories, and an increasingly isolated and frustrated individual delivered over almost entirely to his own caprices.

The egoism governing such love-based families produces few children and, to the degree even that married couples today want children, it seems to Faye less for the sake of sons and daughters to continue the 'line' and more for the sake of a baby to pamper — a sort of adjunct to their consumerism — something like a living toy. Given that the infant is idolized in this way, parents feel little responsibility for disciplining (or 'parenting') him.

Lacking self-control and an ethic of obedience, the child's development is consequently compromised and his socialization neglected. These post-Sixties' families also tend to be short lived, which means children are frequently traumatized by their broken homes, raised by single parents or in stepfamilies, where their intellectual development is stunted and their blood ties confused. However, without stable families and a sense of lineage, all sense of ethnic or national consciousness — or any understanding of why miscegenation and immigration ought to be opposed — are lost. The destruction of stable families, Faye surmises, bears directly on the present social-sexual chaos, the prevailing sense of meaninglessness, and the impending destruction of Europe's racial stock.

Against the sexual liberationists, Faye upholds the model of the bourgeois family, which achieved a workable compromise between individual desire and social/familial preservation (despite the fact that it was, ultimately, the individualism of bourgeois society, in the form of sexual liberation, that eventually terminated this sort of family).

Though, perhaps, no longer sustainable, the stable couples the old bourgeois family structure supported succeeded in privileging familial and communal interests over amorous ones, doing so in ways that favored the long-term welfare of both the couple and the children. Conjugal love, as a result, came to be impressed with friendship, partnership, and habitual attachments, for the couple was defined not as a self-contained amorous symbiosis, but as the pillar of a larger family architecture. This made conjugal love moderate and balanced rather than passionate — sustained by habit, tenderness, interest, care of the children, and *la douceur du foyer*. Sexual desire remained, but in most cases declined in intensity or dissipated in time.

This family structure was also extraordinarily stable. It assured the lineage, raised properly socialized children, respected women, and enjoyed the support of law and custom. There were, of course, compromises and even hypocrisies (as men, for instance, satisfied certain of their libidinal urgings in brothels), but in any case the family, the basic cell of society, was protected — even privileged.

The great irony of sexual liberation and its ensuing destruction of the bourgeois family is that it has obviously not brought greater happiness or freedom, but rather greater alienation and misery. In this spirit, the media now routinely (almost obsessively) sexualizes the universe, but sex has become more virtual than real: there's more pornography, but less children. It seems hardly coincidental that once the 'rights' of desire were emancipated, sex took on a different meaning, the family collapsed, sexual identity got increasingly confused, perversions and transgressions became greater and more serious. As everyone set off in pursuit of an elusive libidinal fulfillment, the population became correspondently more atomized, uprooted, and miscegenated. In France today, 30 percent of all adults are single and there are even reports of a new 'asexuality' — in reaction to the sexualization of everything.

There's a civilization-destroying tragedy here: for once Europeans are deprived of their family lineage, they cease to transmit their cultural and genetic heritage and thus lose all sense of who they are. This is critical to everything else. As the historians Michael Mitterauer and Reinhard Sieder write: 'The family is one of the most archaic forms of social community, and at all times men have used their family as a model for the formation of human societies'. The loss of family stability, and thus the family's loss as society's basic cell, Faye emphasizes, not only dissolves social relations, it brings disorder and makes all tyrannies possible, for once sexual emancipation helps turn society into a highly individualized, Balkanized mass, totalitarianism (not Soviet or Fascist, but U.S. Progressive) becomes increasingly likely.

The Idolization of Homosexuality

Homophilia and feminism are the most important children of the cultural revolution. They share, as such, much of the same ideological baggage that denies biological realities and wars on the family, conforming in this way to the consumerist and homogenizing dictates of the post-Rooseveltian international order that's dominated North America and Western Europe for the last half century or so.

In the late 1960s, when homosexuals began demanding legal equality, Faye claims they were fully within their rights. Homosexuality in his view is a genetic abnormality (affecting less than 5 percent of males) and thus an existential affliction; he thus doesn't object to homosexuals practicing their sexuality within the privacy of their bedrooms. What he finds objectionable is the confusion of private and public realms and the assertion of homophilia as a social norm. Worse, he claims that in much elite discourse, homosexuals have quickly gone from being pariahs to privileged beings, who now flaunt their alleged 'superiority' over heterosexuals, seen as old fashioned, outmoded, ridiculous — like the woman who centers her life on the home and the care of her children rather than on a career — and thus as something bizarre and implicitly opposed to liberal-style 'emancipation'.

Faye, by no means a prude, contends that female homosexuality is considerably different from and less dysgenic than male homosexuality. Most lesbians, in his view, are bisexual, rather than purely homosexual, and for whatever reason have turned against males. This he sees as a reflection on men. Lesbianism also lacks the same negative civilizational consequence as male homosexuality. It rarely shocked traditional societies because women engaging in homosexual relations retained their femininity. Male homosexuality, by contrast, was considered socially abhorrent, for it violated the nature of masculinity, making men no longer 'properly' male and thus something aberrant. (To those who invoke the ancient glories of Athens as a counter-argument, Faye, a long-time Greco-Latinist, says that in the period when a certain form of pederasty was tolerated, no adult Greek ever achieved respectability or standing in his community, if not married, devoted to the interests of his family and clan, and, above all, not 'made of woman' — i.e., sexually penetrated.)

Like feminism, homophilia holds that humans are bisexual at birth and (willfully or not) choose their individual sexual orientation — as if anatomical differences are insignificant and all humans are basically alike, a *tabula rasa* upon which they are to inscribe their self-chosen 'destiny'. This view lacks any scientific credibility, to be sure (even if it is professed in our elite universities), and, like anti-racism, it resembles Lysenkoism in denying those biological realities incompatible with the reigning dogmas. (Facts, though, have rarely stood in the way of faith or ideology — or, in the secular Twentieth century, ideologies that have become religious faiths.)

Even when assuming the mantle of its allegedly progressive and emancipatory pretensions, homophilia, like sexual liberation in general, is entirely self-centered and present-minded, promoting 'lifestyles' hostile to family formation and thus to white reproduction. Here homophilia marches hand in hand with anti-racism, denying the significance of biological differences and the imperatives of white reproduction.

This subversive ideology now even aspires to reinvent homosexuals as the flower of society — liberators preparing the way to joy, liberty, fraternity, tolerance, social well-being, good taste, etc. As vice is transformed into virtue, homosexuality allegedly introduces a new sense of play and gaiety to the one-dimensional society of sad, heterosexual males. Only, Faye insists, there's nothing genuinely gay about the gays, for theirs is a condition of stress and disequilibrium. At odds with their own nature, homosexual sexuality is often a Calvary — and not because of social oppression, but because of those endogenous reasons (particularly their attraction to their own sex) that condemn them to dysgenic behaviors.

In its public display as Gay Pride, homophilia accordingly defines itself as narcissistic, exhibitionist, and infantile — revealing in these characteristics those traits that are perhaps specific to its condition. In any case, a community worthy of itself, Faye tells us, is founded on shared values, on achievements, on origins — but not a dysgenic sexual orientation.

Schizophrenic Feminism

The reigning egalitarianism is always extending itself, trying to force the real — in the realms of sexuality, individuality, demography (race), etc. — to conform to its tenets. The demand that women have the same legal rights and opportunities as men, Faye thinks, was entirely just — especially for Europeans (and especially Celtic, Scandinavian, and Germanic Europeans), for their cultures have long respected the humanity of their women. Indeed, he considers legal equality the single great accomplishment of feminism. But once achieved, feminism has since been transformed into a utopian and delirious neo-egalitarianism that makes sexes, like races, equivalent and interchangeable. There is accordingly no such thing as 'men's work' or 'women's work'. Human dignity and fulfillment, it's held, is possible only in doing something that makes money. Faye, though, refuses to equate legal equality with natural equality, for such an ideological muddling denies obvious biological differences, offending both science and common sense.

The dogma that differences between men and women are simply cultural derives from a feminist behaviorism in which women are seen as potential men and femininity is treated as a social distortion. In Simone de Beauvoir's formulation: One is not born a woman, one becomes one. Feminists, as such, affirm the equality and interchangeability of men and women, yet at the same time they reject femininity, which they consider something inferior and imposed. The feminist model is thus the man, and feminism's New Woman is simply his 'photocopy'. In endeavoring to suppress the specifically feminine in this way, feminism aims to masculinize women and feminize men in the image of its androgynous ideal — analogous to the anti-racist ideal of the *métis* (the mixed race or half-caste). This unisex ideology, in its extremism, characterizes the mother as a slave and the devoted wife as a fool. In practice, it even rejects the biological functions of the female body, aspiring to a masculinism that imitates men and seeks to emulate them socially, politically, and otherwise. Feminism in a word is anti-feminine — anti-mother and anti-family — and ultimately anti-reproduction.

Anatomical differences, however, have consequences. Male humans, like males of other species, always differ from females — given that their biological specification dictates specific behaviors. These human sexual differences may be influenced by culture and other factors. But they nevertheless exist, which means they inevitably affect mind and behavior — despite what the Correctorate wants everyone to believe.

Male superiority in worldly achievement — conceptual, mathematical, artistic, political, and otherwise — has often been explained by female oppression, a notion Faye rejects, though he acknowledges that in many areas of contemporary life, for just or unjust reasons, women do suffer disadvantages — and in many non-white societies outright subjugation. Male physical strength may also enable men to dominate women. But generally, Faye sees a rough equality of intelligence between men and women. Their main differences, he contends, are psychological and characterological, for men tend to be more outwardly oriented than women. As such, they use their intelligence more in competition, innovation, and discovery, linked to the fact that they are usually more aggressive, more competitive, more vain and narcissistic than women — who, by contrast, are more inclined to be emotionally loyal, submissive, prudent, temperate, and far-sighted.

Men and women, though, are better viewed as organic complements, rather than as inferior or superior. From Homer to Cervantes to Mme. de Staël, the image of women, their realms and their work, however diverse and complicated, have differed from that of men. Women may be able to handle most masculine tasks, but at the same time their disposition differs from men, especially in the realm of creativity.

This is critical for Faye. In all sectors of practical intelligence women perform as well as men — but not in their capacity for imaginative projection, which detaches and abstracts one's self from contingent reality for the sake of imagining another. This holds in practically all areas: epic poetry, science, invention, religion, cuisine or design. It is not from female brains, he notes, that there have emerged submarines, space flight, philosophical systems, great political and economic theories, and major scientific discoveries (Mme. Curie being the exception). Most of the great breakthroughs have in fact been made by men and it has had nothing to do with women being oppressed or repressed. Feminine dreams are simply not the same as masculine ones — which search the impossible, the risky, the unreal.

Akin, then, in spirit to homophilia, anti-racism, and Sixties-style sexual liberation, feminism's rejection of biological realities and its effort to masculinize women end up not just distorting what it supposedly champions — women — it reveals the totally egoistic and present-oriented nature of its ideology, which rejects women as mothers and thus rejects the reproduction of the race.

Conclusion

Sexe et dévoiement treats a variety of other issues: Christian and Islamic views on sexuality; immigration and the different sexual practices it brings (some of which are extremely primitive and brutal); the necessary role of prostitution in society; and the effect that new biotechnologies are going to have on sexuality.

From the above discussion — of the family, homophilia, and feminism — the reader should already have a sense of the direction Faye's argument takes, as he relates individual sexuality to certain macrochanges now forcing European civilization off its rails. Because this is an especially illuminating perspective on the decline of the white race (linking demography, civilization, and sex) and one of which there seem too few — I think this lends special pertinence to his essay.

There are not a few historical and methodological criticisms, however, that could be made of *Sexe et dévoiement*, two of which I find especially dissatisfying. Like the European New Right as a whole, he tends to be overly simplistic in attributing to the secularization of certain Christian notions, like equality and love, the origins of the maladies he depicts. Similarly, he refuses to link cultural/ideological influences to social/economic developments (seeing their causal relationship as essentially one-way instead of dialectical), just as he fails to consider the negative effects that America's imperial supremacy, with its post-European rules of behavior and its anti-Christian policies, have had on Europe in the last half century.

But after having said that — and after having reviewed many of Guillaume Faye's works over the last ten years, as well as having read a great many other books in the meantime that have made me more critical of aspects of his thought — I think these 'failings' pale in comparison to the light he sheds on the ethnocidal forces now bearing down on the European race.

American Renaissance, June 29, 2012

13

THE TRANSITIONAL PROGRAM

Apropos of Guillaume Faye, *Mon Programme: Un programme révolutionnaire ne vise pas à changer les règles du jeu mais à changer de jeu.* Chevaigné: Éds. du Lore, 2012.

Following quickly on the heels of *Sexe et dévoiement* (2011), which examined the social-sexual roots of the present European demographic crisis, Faye's latest book is a very different kind of work, addressing quite another, though not entirely unrelated problem.

Theory and Practice

When dealing with political ideas in the largest sense (i.e., as they bear on the life or death of the *polis*), there comes a time, he argues, when critical and analytical thought, with its commentaries and opinions, has to pass from the abstract to the concrete. The most brilliant medical diagnosis, to give an analogy, is worth little if it does not eventually lead to a curative therapy.

In this vein, his *Programme* represents an effort to pass from the theoretical to the practical, as it proposes certain concrete policies (political therapies) to treat the ills presently afflicting the French state — and by extension, other European states. The details of this program make little reference to the American situation, but its general principles speak to the malignancy infecting all states of the Americanosphere.

Reform and Revolution

Faye's program is not, ostensibly, about reforming the existing state. That would only 'improve' a political system, whose corruptions, vices, and totalitarian powers are increasingly immune to correction. The state's lack of authority and democratic legitimacy, combined with the entrenchment of the New Class interests controlling it, means that such a system cannot actually be changed in any significant way. Hence the claim of Faye's subtitle: A Revolutionary Program (i.e., one that attacks the existing disorder at its roots) Does Not Aim at Changing the Rules of the Game But at Changing the Game Itself. The 'game' here is the existing political system, which has become an obvious catastrophe for European peoples. For every patriot, this system needs not to be changed, but to be razed and rebuilt — from the ground up and according to an entirely different paradigm.

There is, though, a certain terminological confusion in the way Faye describes his program. He realizes it is something of a pipe dream. No state or party is likely to embrace it — though, of course, this does not lessen the value of its exercise, nor does it mean it will not fertilize future projects of a similar sort. We also do not know what is coming and perhaps there will be a moment of breakdown — Joseph Tainter's 'Collapse' — making possible a revolutionary transition. If, then, 'we' should ever have the occasion to assume power and restructure the state: how would we go about it?

Faye's *Programme* is an effort to start thinking about such an alternative in a situation where a regime-threatening crisis of one sort or another brings a 'new majority' to power. He doesn't specifically spell out what such a crisis might entail, but it is easily imaginable. In 2017, for example, if the present society-destroying problems of unemployment, deindustrialization, massive indebtedness, uncontrolled Third World immigration, etc., are not fixed, and nothing suggests that they will, an anti-system party, like the National Front, could conceivably be voted into power. (The situation in Greece, as I write, borders on the pre-revolutionary.) In such a situation a new majority might submit something like his *Programme* to a referendum, calling on the 'people' to authorize a radical restructuring of the political system.

I can think of at least two national revolutions that came to power in a similar institutional (legal) way: the Sinn Féin MPs of December

1918 who refused to sit at Westminster and the NSDAP coalition that
got a chance to form a government in January 1933.

The *Programme* anticipates a less catastrophic situation than foreseen in his *Convergence des catastrophes* (2004) or implied in *Avant-
Guerre* (2002). Perhaps he is suggesting that this scenario is more real-
istic or likely now; I'm not certain. But it is strange to see so little of his
convergence theory — what Tainter calls the ever mounting costliness
of complexity — in his program, especially while positing a crisis as
the program's premise.

In any case, his *Programme* assumes its political remediation will
be administered before the present system collapses, at a moment
when a new majority gets a chance to form a government from the
debris of the old. For this reason, I think it is better characterized as
'transitional' (in the Trotskyist sense).

Unlike a revolutionary program that outlines a strategy for overturning the existing order and seizing state power, a transitional
program addresses a crisis in terms of the existing institutional
parameters, but does so in ways that reach beyond their limits and
are unacceptable to the ruling powers — challenging the system's logic
and thus posing a threat to its 'order'. (See Leon Trotsky, *The Death
Agony of Capitalism and the Tasks of the Fourth International* [1938].)

The State

In *The Politics*, Aristotle conceives of the state almost organically: the
head of a body (the *polis*) — the political system that rules the City and
ensures order within its measured boundaries.

In his self-consciously Aristotelian approach — which favors individual liberty, responsibility, hierarchy, and ethno-cultural homogeneity — Faye's program aims at lessening the state's costly, inefficient
administrative functions, enhancing its sovereign powers, and abandoning its appropriation of functions that properly belong to the family and society.

This entails freeing the French state from the present European
Union (whose Orwellian stranglehold on Continental life is objectively anti-European). He does not actually advocate withdrawing
from it, but rather refusing to cooperate with it until its rules are rede-
signed and national sovereignty is restored. Given that France is the
most politically significant of the European states and is pivotal to

the EU's existence, it has the power to force a major revamping of its policies and restore something of the European Idea that inspired the original Treaty of Rome (1958).

If achieved, this restoration of national sovereignty would imbue the French state with the freedom to remodel its institutions — not for the sake of undermining the primacy of the state, as our libertarians would have it, but of excising its cancers and enhancing its 'regalian' will to 're-establish, preserve, and develop the identity, the prosperity, the security, and the power of France and Europe'.

Faye is not a traditional French nationalist, but a Europeanist favoring Continental unity (an imperial family of nations rather than a global marketplace). He believes both the French state and the EU have a liberal-socialist concept of the political, which makes them unable to distinguish between their friends and enemies — given that the individualist, universalistic, and pluralist postulates of their ideology views the world in market and moralist terms, holding that only matters of ethics and economics are primary. (In traditional, organic civilizations it is the Holy that is primary.)

A restoration of sovereignty would give the French state the freedom to restructure and rebuild itself.

Globally, he proposes measures that would control the nation's borders, revitalize its national economy, improve its efficiency, reduce its costs, amputate its nomenclature, streamline its functions, and concentrate on the national interest, and not, like now, on the special interests. But there is nothing in the *Programme* that would mobilize the French themselves for the transition. It is a strictly top-down project that ignores what Patrick Pearse called 'the sovereign people', who are vital to the success of every revolutionary movement.

The state, in any case, is too large — which is true almost everywhere. At its top and bottom, its functions and personnel need to be greatly reduced — cabinet positions should be reduced to six (Defense, Justice, Foreign Affairs, Interior, Economy, and Instruction/ Patrimony) and the number of state functionaries cut by at least 50 percent. Faye's proposals would remove cumbersome, over-regulating, and counterproductive state agencies for the sake of freeing up funds for more worthwhile investments in the private sector.

Toward these ends, he proposes overturning the anti-democratic role of judges, who in the name of the Constitution thwart the popular will (constitutional questions would be left to the Senate); introducing referendums that give the electorate a greater say in major policy decisions; restoring popular liberties, like the right to free speech; introducing 'positive' law that judges the crime and not the criminal; abolishing the privileges of higher state functionaries (now greater than those of the Eighteenth-century aristocracy); and eliminating the present confusion of state powers.

The Economy

In the modern world, the power (in a material sense) of a nation-state is in its economy. (The health and longevity of the nation — in the spiritual sense — is another thing, dependent on its demography, the preservation of its genetic heritage, the quality of its culture, and the culture's transmission.)

Though conscious of the dangers posed by economism, Faye believes 'prosperity' is necessary (though not sufficient) for social harmony and national defense. Politics and economics are different realms, operating according to different logics. But he rejects both the Marxist contention that the state's political economy can do anything it wishes in the market and the liberal-conservative position that it can do nothing. Straddling the two, he advocates a political economy whose guiding principles are non-ideological and pragmatic: 'What counts is what works — not what conforms to a dogma'. Sound economic practice, in other words, is based on experience, not theory.

The great financial crisis of 2008, whose ravages are still evident, was not, he claims, a crisis of capitalism, but a crisis of the welfare state — and thus a crisis of 'statism' (*étatisme*). The crippling state debt allegedly at the root of this crisis stems, he argues, from the state's profligate spending, its ever-growing number of functionaries, its bureaucratic mismanagement and cronyism, and its unsupportable social charges, like the Afro-Arab hordes occupying its *banlieues*. Left-wing talk of 'ultra-liberalism' is delusional in economies as regulated as those of Europe. In living beyond its means, the state has acquired debts it cannot afford and now blames it on others.

Faye dismisses those who claim the crisis was created by a conspiracy of banksters and vampire capitalists. Targeting solely the failures of the present political system, he does not see or think it is important that there is something of a revolving door (perhaps greater in the U.S. than France) between the state and the corporations, that the crimes of the money powers are intricately linked to state policies, and thus that the economic interests have had not only a corrupting and distorting effect on the state, but in many cases have subsumed the powers of the state. (As I write, two European governments have been taken over by agents of Goldman Sachs.) In his anti-Marxism, Faye is wont to stress the primacy of the 'superstructure', rather than the economic 'base' (which, most of the time, is probably a reliable rule of thumb). Similarly, he does not relate the current crisis to globalization, which has everywhere undermined the existing models of governance, nor does he consider the often nefarious role played by the IMF, the WTO, and the new global oligarchs. He blames the crisis solely on the state's incompetent and spendthrift policies, leaving blameless the moneylenders and criminals, whose bailout raised the national debt beyond any possible repayment. The state may be primary to a people's existence, but in the neo-liberal regimes of the West, it is clearly subordinated to the dominant economic interests. The two (state and economy) seem hardly understandable except in relation to one another — though he wants us to believe the cause of the crisis was purely political. (In my mind, it is civilizational.)

In any case, the French state is over-administrated, 'socialist' in effect; it has too many workers (almost 25 percent of the workforce); it pursues social-engineering domestically and economy-destroying free trade policies internationally — the most self-destructive policies conceivable. Given capitalism's quantitative logic, the state's globalist free trade policies are also destroying Europe's ability to compete with low-wage Third World economies, like China, and are thus devastating the productive capacity of its economies. France and Europe, Faye argues, need to protect themselves from the ravages of global free trade by creating a Eurasian autarkic economic zone, from Galway to Vladivostok (what he once called 'Euro-Siberia', though there's no mention of it here) — and at the same time they need to liberalize their domestic economies by throwing off excessive regulations and social charges for the sake of unleashing European initiative and enterprise. He calls thus for changes in the EU that focus on stimulating the European market rather than allowing it to succumb to America's global market, which is turning the Continent's advanced economies into financialized and tertiarized economies, unable to provide decent paying jobs or promote national and class solidarity. The emphasis of his program is thus on national economic growth.

The present policy of budget austerity, he argues, is compounding the crisis, causing state revenues to decline and forcing the economy into depression. Growth alone will generate the wealth needed to get out of debt. To this end, the state needs to radically cut costs, but do so without imposing austerity measures. This entails not just simplifying and rationalizing public functions, but changing the underlying paradigm. The state should not, therefore, indiscriminately reduce public expenses, but rather suppress useless, unproductive charges, while augmenting wealth-creating ones. Basically, he wants the state to withdraw from the economy, but without abandoning its role in protecting the public and national interests. For those key sectors vital to the nation's economy and security — energy, armaments, aerospace, and high tech — the state should exercise a certain strategic control over them, but without interfering in their management. He also calls for a tax revolution that will unburden the middle class and expand the tax base. Similarly, he wants the state to encourage enterprise by relieving business of costly social charges, especially on small and middle-size enterprises that create employment; he wants the French to work more — increasing the workweek from 35 hours to 40, and decreasing annual vacations from five weeks to four; he wants a liberalization of the labor market, with a system of national preferences favoring French workers over immigrants; he wants a different system of unemployment benefits that encourages work and rationalizes job placements; he wants a cap on executive salaries and an end to golden parachutes; and he wants state subventions of public worker unions discontinued, along with their right to strike.

As a general principle, he claims the state should not grant rights it cannot afford, that those who can work should, that foreigners have no right to public services (including education), that quotas imposing artificial forms of sexual and racial equality are intolerable, and that only natives unable to work should be entitled to public assistance. Social justice, he observes, is not a matter of socialist redistribution, but of a system whose pragmatic efficiencies and competitive industries are able to provide for the nation's needs. There are, however, no proposals in his program for reindustrialization, state economic planning, or an alternative form of economy based on something other than capitalism's incessant need to grow and consume.

Closely related to the country's economic problems is that of the state's failed *politique familiale*. The state, he argues, needs to adopt measures to offset the social problems created by exploding divorce rates and declining birthrates. The aging of the population is also going to require increased medical services, which need to be expanded and improved. As for the rising generation, he calls for a revamping of the national education system, which has become a 'cretin-producing factory'. Although France's Third Republic had one of the finest educational systems in the world, that of the Fifth Republic has been an utter disaster, due largely to Left-wing egalitarian policies catering to the lowest common dominator (the Barbarians within the Gates).

The state, moreover, has no right to 'educate' youth — that is totalitarian and the role of the family (and, I would add, the Church). The state should instead provide schools that instruct — that convey knowledge and its methods — not inculcate the reigning Left ideologies. Discipline must also be restored; all violence and disorder in schools must be severely punished. Immigrants and non-natives ought to be excluded. Obligatory schooling should end at age 14, and a system of apprenticeship (like that of Germany) should be made available to those who do not pursue academic degrees. The universities also need to be revamped, with more rigorous forms of instruction, dress codes, tracking, and the elimination of such frivolous disciplines as psychology, sociology, communications, advertising, etc. There are, though, no proposed measures in his program to strengthen the nation's ethno-cultural identity, resist the audio-visual imperialism of America's entertainment industry, or outlaw CIA-funded NGOs.

Immigration

The present soft totalitarian ideology of the French state, like states throughout the Americanosphere, portrays immigration as an 'enrichment', though obviously it is everywhere and in all ways a disaster, threatening the nation's ethnic fundament, its standard of living, and its cultural integrity. Immigration is also code for Third World colonization and Islamization.

Against those claiming it is impossible to stem the immigrant tide, Faye contends that what is needed is a will to do so — a will to eliminate the 'pull' factors (like welfare) that attract the immigrant invaders. He proposes zero immigration, the deportation of illegals, the expulsion of unemployed legal ones, the end to family 'reunions', the strict policing of student and tourist visas, the abolition of asylum rights, visa controls on international transportation links, the elimination of state-funded social assistance to foreigners, national preference in employment, and the replacement of *jus soli* by *jus sanguinis*.

Given that Muslims are a special threat, Faye proposes abolishing all state-supported Muslim associations, prohibiting mosque building and halal practices, imposing heavy fines on veiled women, eliminating Muslim chaplains from the military and the prison system, and implementing a general policy of restrictive legislation toward Islam. Surprisingly, he proposes no measures to break up the non-European ghettos presently sponging off French taxpayers and constituting a highly destabilizing factor within the body politic (perhaps because the above measures would prevent these ghettos from continuing to exist).

Even these relatively moderate measures, he realizes, are likely to stir up trouble, for every positive action inevitably comes with its negative effects. But unless measures aimed at stopping the 'pull' factors promoting the immigrant invasion are taken, Faye warns, it may be too late for France, in which case more drastic measures will have to be taken later — and Plan B will have no pity.

The World

The state's defense of the nation and its relationship with other states are two of its most defining functions.

To those familiar with Faye's earlier thoughts on these subjects, they will find the same general orientation — a rejection of Atlanticism, a realignment with Russia, neutrality to the U.S., withdrawal from the Third World, and armed vigilance toward Islam. His stance on NATO, the U.S., and Russia, though, is more 'moderate' than those he has taken in the past.

The *Programme* depicts the present EU as objectively anti-European, but does not call for an outright withdrawal from it. It similarly recognizes that NATO subordinates Europe to America's destructive crusades and alliances (impinging on the basic principle of sovereignty: the right to declare war) and again does not call for a withdrawal, only a strategy to diminish its significance. And, finally, though he thinks Russia should be the axis of French policy (which is indeed her only viable geopolitical option), there is little in his program that would advance the prospects of such a realignment or help realign France against the surreptitious war of encirclement presently being waged by the U.S. against Russia. There is also nothing on the present 'unipolar-to-multipolar phase' of international politics, brought on by America's imperial decline — as it goes about threatening war and international havoc, all the while supremely indifferent to the collapse of its own economic fundamentals. On these key policies related to France's position in the world, he stands to the 'Right' of Marine Le Pen.

Faye's program aims mainly at restoring French sovereignty, but, as suggested, on issues relevant to its restoration, his position would greatly modify France's submission to the anti-sovereign powers, not break with them. At the root of this apparent irresolution, I suspect, is his understanding of Islam. Faye has long designated it as Europe's principal enemy. And there is no question that Islam, as a civilization, is objectively and threateningly anti-European, and that Muslim immigrants pose a dire threat to France's future. But his half-right position has taken him down a wayward path: to an alliance with Islam's great enemy, Israel, and to an accommodation with Israel's Guardian Angel, the United States, the world's foremost anti-white power. For it is the American system (in arming and abetting jihadists to destabilize regimes it seeks to control) that has made Islam such a world threat, and it is the American system (in the blight of its leveling commercialism and the poisonous vapors of its human rights ideology) that poses the greatest, most profound threat to European existence.

Faye's questionable position on these issues, more generally, comes from ignoring the nature of the post-1945 *nomos* imposed by New York-Washington on a defeated Europe and the rest of the non-Communist world. America has always had an ambivalent relationship to Europe — being both an offshoot of European Christian civilization and a Puritan (in effect, Bolshevik) opponent of it. Since the end of the last world war — when it formally threw off the Christian moral foundations of the last thousand years of European civilization by morally sanctioning 'the destruction of residential areas and the mass killing of civilians as a routine method of warfare' — a new counter-civilization, an empire of liberty and chaos, has come to rule the world (even if during the 45 years of the Cold War the U.S. encouraged the illusion that it was a bastion of Western values and Christianity). (See Desmond Fennell, *The Postwestern Condition: Between Chaos and Civilization* [1999]; Carl Schmitt, *The Nomos of the Earth* [2006 (1950)].)

Not just the devastated Germans and Italians, but all postwar Europeans were subsequently integrated into the predatory empire of this counter-civilization — and subjected to its transvaluation of values (consumerism, permissiveness, abortion, the elimination of sex differences, the death of God, the end of art, anti-racism, and the 'newspeak' whose inversions hold that 'war is peace', 'dictatorship is democracy', 'ignorance is culture', etc.). European elites have since become not just a comprador bourgeoisie, but home-grown exemplars of the moral and cultural void (the Thanatos principle) animating the American system. It is, arguably, this system and its poisons that have made Europeans indifferent to their survival as a people and accounts for the increasing dysfunctionality of their established institutions — not the mass influx of Third World immigrants, who are a (prominent and very unpleasant) symptom, though not the source, of the reigning inversions.

Without acknowledging this, Faye can argue that America is only an adversary of Europe — a power that might exploit Europeans, but not one posing a life and death threat to their existence, like a true enemy. He forgets, accordingly, that America and America's special friend, Britain, rather consciously destroyed historic Europe — that civilization born from the 'medieval' alliance of Charlemagne and the Papacy. During the course of its anti-fascist crusade, the imperial leviathan headquartered in New York-Washington threw off the values and forms of Europe's venerable Christian civilization for ones based on the *sanctioning of mass murder.*

Such premises have since inspired its ongoing campaigns 'to abolish and demolish and derange' the world. This system is what most endangers white people today — for it wars on everything refusing to bend to its 'liberal democratic' (i.e., money driven) colonization, standardization, and demeaning of private and social life — as it breaks up traditional communities, isolates the individual within an increasingly indifferent 'global order' dismissive of history, culture, and nature, rejects historically and religiously established sources of meaning, and leaves in their stead innumerable worthless consumer items and a whorl of fabricated electronic simulacra that situate all life within its hyperreal bubble. Even in an indirect or transitional way, Faye does not address this most eminent of the anti-European forces, offering no real alternative to the U.S./EU consumer paradise, whose present breakdown will be recuperated only by a resistance whose political vision transcends the underlying tenets of the existing one.

Conclusion

As an exercise, Faye's *Programme* displays much of its author's characteristic intelligence and creativity, and it stands as a respectable complement to the numerous interpretative and analytical works he has written on various aspects of European life over the last decade and a half—works written with verve and an imagination rich in imagery, lucidity, and urgency. As a brief programmatic redefinition of the French state system, his program is also, admittedly, impressive. It is not, however, revolutionary. In some respects, it is not transitional. Above all, it does not get at the roots of the existing disorder: the satanic system that is presently destroying both Europe and the remnants of European civilization in America.

If Faye continues to speak for the rising forces of European identitarianism and populism, he will need to invent a better 'game' than his program—for what seems most needed in this period of transition is a worldview premised on the overthrow of the existing *nomos*.

Counter-Currents, August 28, 2012

Appendix
The Books of Guillaume Faye

Le Système à tuer les peuples. Paris: Copernic, 1981.

La Nouvelle société de consommation. Paris: Le Labyrinthe, 1983.

Contre l'économisme: Principes de l'économie politique. Paris: Le Labyrinthe, 1983.

Sexe et idéologie. Paris: Le Labyrinthe, 1984.

L'Occident comme déclin. Paris: Le Labyrinthe, 1985.

Avant-Guerre (graphic novel). Paris: Carrère, 1985.

Nouveau discours à la nation européenne. Paris: Albatros, 1985; revised second edition, Paris: L'Æncre, 1999.

Les Nouveaux enjeux idéologiques. Paris: Le Labyrinthe, 1985.

Le Guide de l'engueulade (in collaboration with Jean-Philippe Serrano). Paris: Presses de la Cité, 1992.

Le Manuel du séducteur pressé (in collaboration with Jean-Philippe Serrano). Paris: Presses de la Cité, 1993.

L'Archéofuturisme. Paris: L'Æncre, 1998. Translated by Sergio Knipe as *Archeofuturism: European Visions of the Post-Catastrophe Age* (London: Arktos, 2010).

Les Extraterrestres de A à Z. Paris: Dualpha, 2000.

La Colonisation de l'Europe: Discours vrai sur l'immigration et l'Islam. Paris: L'Æncre, 2000.

Pourquoi nous combattons: Manifeste de la résistance européenne. Paris: L'Æncre, 2001. Translated by Michael O'Meara as *Why We Fight: Manifesto of the European Resistance* (London: Arktos, 2011).

Avant-Guerre: Chronique d'un cataclysme annoncé. Paris: L'Æncre, 2002.

La Convergence des catastrophes (under the pseudonym Guillaume Corvus). Paris: Diffusion International, 2004. Translated by E. Christian Kopff as *Convergence of Catastrophes* (London: Arktos, 2012).

Chirac contre les fachos (graphic novel, illustrated by Chard). Paris: GFA, 2004.

Le Coup d'État mondial: Essai sur le Nouvel Impérialisme Américain. Paris: L'Æncre, 2004.

La Nouvelle question juive. Chevaigné: Éds. du Lore, 2007.

Sexe et dévoiement. Chevaigné: Éds. du Lore, 2011.

Mon Programme: Un programme révolutionnaire ne vise pas à changer les règles du jeu mais à changer de jeu. Chevaigné: Éds. du Lore, 2012.

L'Archéofuturisme V2.0: Nouvelles cataclysmiques. Chevaigné: Éds. du Lore, 2012.

Other titles published by Arktos:

Beyond Human Rights
by Alain de Benoist

Manifesto for a European Renaissance
by Alain de Benoist & Charles Champetier

The Problem of Democracy
by Alain de Benoist

Germany's Third Empire
by Arthur Moeller van den Bruck

The Arctic Home in the Vedas
by Bal Gangadhar Tilak

Revolution from Above
by Kerry Bolton

The Fourth Political Theory
by Alexander Dugin

Fascism Seen from the Right
by Julius Evola

Metaphysics of War
by Julius Evola

The Path of Cinnabar
by Julius Evola

Archeofuturism
by Guillaume Faye

Convergence of Catastrophes
by Guillaume Faye

Why We Fight
by Guillaume Faye

The WASP Question
by Andrew Fraser

War and Democracy
by Paul Gottfried

The Saga of the Aryan Race
by Porus Homi Havewala

Homo Maximus
by Lars Holger Holm

The Owls of Afrasiab
by Lars Holger Holm

De Naturae Natura
by Alexander Jacob

Fighting for the Essence
by Pierre Krebs

Can Life Prevail?
by Pentti Linkola

The Ten Commandments of Propaganda
by Brian Anse Patrick

A Handbook of Traditional Living
by Raido

The Agni and the Ecstasy
by Steven J. Rosen

The Jedi in the Lotus
by Steven J. Rosen

It Cannot Be Stormed
by Ernst von Salomon

Tradition & Revolution
by Troy Southgate

Against Democracy and Equality
by Tomislav Sunic

The Initiate: Journal of Traditional Studies
by David J. Wingfield (ed.)

Lightning Source UK Ltd.
Milton Keynes UK
UKOW04f0143190316

270488UK00006B/246/P